10 years of the LLAS elearning symposium: case studies in good practice

Edited by Kate Borthwick,
Erika Corradini and Alison Dickens

Published by Research-publishing.net, not-for-profit association
Dublin, Ireland; Voillans, France, info@research-publishing.net

© 2015 by Research-publishing.net (collective work)
Each author retains their own copyright

10 years of the LLAS elearning symposium: case studies in good practice
Edited by Kate Borthwick, Erika Corradini, & Alison Dickens

Rights: All articles in this collection are published under the Attribution-NonCommercial -NoDerivatives 4.0 International (CC BY-NC-ND 4.0) licence. Under this licence, the contents are freely available online (as PDF files) for anybody to read, download, copy, and redistribute provided that the author(s), editorial team, and publisher are properly cited. Commercial use and derivative works are, however, not permitted.

Disclaimer: Research-publishing.net does not take any responsibility for the content of the pages written by the authors of this book. The authors have recognised that the work described was not published before, or that it is not under consideration for publication elsewhere. While the information in this book are believed to be true and accurate on the date of its going to press, neither the editorial team, nor the publisher can accept any legal responsibility for any errors or omissions that may be made. The publisher makes no warranty, expressed or implied, with respect to the material contained herein. While Research-publishing.net is committed to publishing works of integrity, the words are the authors' alone.

Trademark notice: product or corporate names may be trademarks or registered trademarks, and are used only for identification and explanation without intent to infringe.

Copyrighted material: every effort has been made by the editorial team to trace copyright holders and to obtain their permission for the use of copyrighted material in this book. In the event of errors or omissions, please notify the publisher of any corrections that will need to be incorporated in future editions of this book.

Typeset by Research-publishing.net
Cover design and frog picture by Raphaël Savina
Illustration of the retro-themed birthday greetings (id# 129712892) by "© Hermin/www.shutterstock.com"

ISBN13: 978-1-908416-22-3 (Paperback - Print on demand, black and white)
Print on demand technology is a high-quality, innovative and ecological printing method; with which the book is never 'out of stock' or 'out of print'.

ISBN13: 978-1-908416-23-0 (Ebook, PDF, colour)
ISBN13: 978-1-908416-24-7 (Ebook, EPUB, colour)

Legal deposit, Ireland: The National Library of Ireland, The Library of Trinity College, The Library of the University of Limerick, The Library of Dublin City University, The Library of NUI Cork, The Library of NUI Maynooth, The Library of University College Dublin, The Library of NUI Galway.

Legal deposit, United Kingdom: The British Library.
British Library Cataloguing-in-Publication Data.
A cataloguing record for this book is available from the British Library.

Legal deposit, France: Bibliothèque Nationale de France - Dépôt légal: janvier 2015.

Table of contents

vi	Notes on contributors
xiv	Acknowledgements
xv	Foreword
1	10 years of the LLAS elearning symposium: An introduction *Kate Borthwick, Erika Corradini, and Alison Dickens*

Section 1. Language learning in new contexts: mobile learning

11	A journey to the East? Trials and tribulations of a personal journey with technology and languages *Marion Sadoux*
21	Technological diversity: A case study into language learners' mobile technology use inside and outside the classroom *Billy Brick and Tiziana Cervi-Wilson*
31	Podcasting as a language teaching and learning tool *Fernando Rosell-Aguilar*

Section 2. Collaboration and open learning

43	A reflective e-learning journey from the dawn of CALL to web 2.0 intercultural communicative competence (ICC) *Marina Orsini-Jones*
57	Learning to swim in new waters: A meta-narrative about the design and implementation of a virtual learning environment for language learning and teaching *Teresa MacKinnon*

Table of contents

67   From autonomous to peer e-learning – How the FReE Team turned ePortfolio into a social network between first and final-year modern languages students
     Jean-Christophe Penet

77   OER (re)use and language teachers' tacit professional knowledge: Three vignettes
     Tita Beaven

89   Dyslexia in modern language learning: A case study on collaborative task-design for inclusive teaching and learning in an online context
     Anna Motzo and Debora Quattrocchi

Section 3. Fostering creativity in the classroom

105 Reflections on a personal journey in learning design
     Julie Watson

117 Collaborative production of learning objects on French literary works using the LOC software
     Christine Penman

127 Digital English – me, online, writing & academia
     Ania Rolińska

139 The grammar movie project
     Edith Kreutner

151 Tapping technology in creating product development studies: Reflections on an ESP-business project
     Aiden Yeh

163 Using Blackboard Wiki pages as a shared space for simulating the professional translation work environment
Juliet Vine

Section 4. New tools, new practices

175 Connected language learning: A tutor's perspective
Benoît Guilbaud

185 The e-learning tool Voxopop and its benefits on oral skills: Activities for final year students of German
Sascha Stollhans

193 Sound literature: The pedagogy of reconnection through student-authored audiobooks in the Spanish curriculum
Susana Lorenzo-Zamorano

203 Learning foreign languages with ClipFlair: Using captioning and revoicing activities to increase students' motivation and engagement
Rocío Baños and Stavroula Sokoli

215 FLAX: Flexible and open corpus-based language collections development
Alannah Fitzgerald, Shaoqun Wu, and María José Marín

228 Name index

Notes on contributors

Editors

Kate Borthwick is a Senior Academic Coordinator for elearning within the Centre for Languages, Linguistics and Area Studies. She is an experienced developer of online learning materials and an e-tutor and currently coordinates LLAS activity in relation to elearning, including running the annual elearning symposium. She has managed a number of projects related to OER and oversees two repositories of OER for LLAS: LanguageBox and HumBox. She advises on the online development for the University of Southampton's MLANG course, manages the annual online pre-sessional courses, and was the course designer for the University of Southampton/British Council FutureLearn MOOC: 'Understanding Language: learning and teaching.' Her research interests include OER and learning design.

Erika Corradini is an academic coordinator within the Centre for Languages, Linguistics and Area Studies. Erika's research work is centred on the transformations that languages are subject to throughout history with a special focus on English and its cognates. Before coming to LLAS in 2009, Erika lectured in History of the English Language and Early English Texts and taught modern and old languages. At LLAS, Erika manages projects in the areas of translation and interpreting, community languages, multilingualism, and languages in schools and higher education. She assists in coordination of the LLAS elearning symposium and has been involved in LLAS projects related to OER, focussing on copyright and IPR issues in open access. She tweets at @eri_llas.

Alison Dickens is Assistant Director of the Centre for Languages, Linguistics and Area Studies. Alison is a modern linguist who has worked in education for 25 years in a range of language teaching, academic development and project management roles. She currently directs the LLAS academic development programme, develops and delivers training in a number of areas including elearning, language teaching and internationalisation. She was part of the founding team who oversaw the first elearning symposium and has been involved with all subsequent events. She is Deputy Director of Enterprise within Modern Languages at the University of Southampton, and manages the university's language courses within the LifeLong Learning programme.

Invited contributors

Benoît Guilbaud is a Senior French language tutor and course co-ordinator at the University of Manchester in the United Kingdom. He has worked in Higher Education since 2007 after studying and training at the universities of Clermont-Ferrand (France) and Cardiff (UK). He has taught on modules in French for medicine, business and law, as well as general French language. He has presented at a number of conferences on the topics of language teaching, digital literacy and networked learning. He was voted 'Most Innovative Lecturer' at the Manchester Student Union Teaching Awards 2014. He tweets as @BenGuilbaud.

Marina Orsini-Jones is Course Director for the MA in English Language Teaching in the Department of English and Languages at Coventry University where she also coordinates the Scholarship of Teaching and Learning Network in the Faculty of Business, Environment and Society. She has published work on e-learning innovation, language awareness, CALL, digital literacies and e-portfolio-supported personal development planning. She has delivered numerous papers on e-language learning at national and international conferences and organised various e-learning workshops in collaboration with staff at LLAS. She is currently investigating the features of Intercultural Communicative Competence (ICC) in Computer Mediated Communication (CMC).

Marion Sadoux, a passionate linguist, graduated in French and Italian at UCL and also studied Portuguese 'on the side'. In 1991 she joined the UCL Language Centre as it first opened and contributed to the development of its Institution Wide Language Programme (IWLP). After 16 years, she took over the Direction of the London Metropolitan University IWLP and then joined the

Notes on contributors

University of Nottingham in Ningbo in March 2013, as Director of the Language Centre. Her current research interests are theoretical and pedagogical and they are concerned with the use of digital tools to enhance the processes of second language acquisition.

Julie Watson is principal teaching fellow in elearning, in Modern Languages at the University of Southampton. She teaches elearning and also leads eLanguages, a research and development group, creating online resources and distance online courses for use within the university and for commercial purposes. Her main research interest is in learning design and the effective use of new technologies in blended learning.

Contributors

Rocío Baños is Lecturer in Translation at the Centre for Translation Studies (CenTraS) at UCL, where she teaches Audiovisual Translation and Translation Technology. She holds a PhD from the University of Granada, focused on dubbing. Her main research interests lie in the fields of Translation Training, Translation Technology and Audiovisual Translation, especially in dubbing. She has published various articles in these areas, both in English and in Spanish. She is also interested in the potential of audiovisual translation in foreign language learning (FLL). From 2011 to 2014 she took part in the ClipFlair project, on FLL through subtitling and revoicing.

Tita Beaven is a Senior Lecturer in Spanish at the Open University, where she is currently Head of the Department of Languages. Her research interests centre on Open Educational Resources and practices, and in the use of technology in language teaching and learning.

Billy Brick is Languages Centre Manager and principal lecturer in the Department of English and Languages at Coventry University. He is a member of the Faculty of Business, Environment and Society BES Scholarship of Teaching and Learning (SoTL) Network which aims to promote good practice

Notes on contributors

and innovation in teaching and learning within the BES disciplines. He teaches Multimedia in Language Teaching and Learning and Computer Assisted Language Learning. His research interests include Digital Literacies; Social Networking Sites and Language Learning; and Mobile Assisted Language Learning.

Tiziana Cervi-Wilson is a Senior Lecturer and the coordinator for the IWLP and career and employability modules for the English and Languages Department at Coventry University. She teaches all the Italian modules at all levels. She is Co-Project Leader for the Routes into Languages Project for the West Midlands Consortium at Coventry University. She is also a member of the Faculty of Business, Environment and Society BES Scholarship of Teaching and Learning (SoTL) Network. She is interested in Language learning and teaching, Digital literacy in language learning, Multimedia and Computer Assisted Language Learning.

Alannah Fitzgerald is an open education practitioner and researcher working in the area of technology-enhanced English language education. Alannah is also a doctoral candidate in Educational Technology at Concordia University in Montreal, Canada and a member of the Global Open Educational Resources (OER) Graduate Network (GO-GN). Her doctoral thesis research with the FLAX language project, supported by The International Research Foundation (TIRF) for English Language Education and the OER Research Hub at the UK Open University (OU), is investigating the design, development and evaluation of flexible open language resources for uses in informal online learning and in traditional face-to-face classroom-based learning.

Edith Kreutner is a teaching associate at the School of Modern Languages, University of Bristol. After completing her Masters at Innsbruck University and a venture into American Studies for her PhD, her dominant research interests now lie within the field of language acquisition and language pedagogy.

Susana Lorenzo-Zamorano is Senior Language Teaching & Learning Coordinator at the University of Manchester, and an Associate Lecturer for the Open University. She has been a Fellow of the Higher Education Academy since 2011. The focus of her doctoral thesis was contemporary Spanish theatre with special attention to women playwrights and issues on language, gender and performance. Her research interests include intercultural pedagogy and the third space applied to languages, education for sustainable development, enquiry-based learning, interdisciplinarity, distance learning and open educational resources. Susana is a member of the AVALON project (Access to Virtual and Action Learning Live Online).

Teresa MacKinnon is an award winning teacher with a wealth of expertise in online delivery. She is experienced in education management and course design in secondary and higher education. Fellow of Warwick's Institute of Advanced Teaching and Learning and Associate Fellow of the HEA, Teresa has extensive experience of computer-assisted language learning and computer-mediated communication. An exponent of the importance of high quality language teaching in the UK, she was involved in the development of the National Language Standards (now National Occupational Standards) and delivered specialist input into the Ofqual Vocational awards review. Teresa is Vice Chair for external engagement and communications on the University Council for Modern Languages executive. Her twitter presence as @warwicklanguage has over 2,600 followers.

María José Marín has been a lecturer at the English Department of the University of Murcia, Spain, since 2009. She holds a PhD in Corpus Linguistics and English for Specific Purposes (ESP) and has published several articles in scientific journals such as *Corpora, Procedia, Miscelánea: A Journal of English and American Studies or ESP-World*. Her research fields are ESP, legal English, Corpus Linguistics and Applied Linguistics. She is currently lecturing on English as an instrumental and specialised language and Applied Linguistics. María José has also visited the universities of Oslo, Portsmouth and Limerick as a guest researcher.

Anna Motzo is a Lecturer in Languages (Italian) at the Department of Languages at The Open University, UK. She has spent more than fifteen years teaching

Notes on contributors

Italian to students both in Italy and in the UK. Her main area of interest is the development of language learning materials within a technology-enhanced environment and the wider role of e-learning in the democratisation of culture. She is Member of the Italian Committee (Association for Language Learning) and a regular contributor to the Journal *Tuttitalia*. She is currently co-writing the new edition of *Andante*, the OU Beginners Italian multimedia course and chairs *Vivace*, the OU intermediate Italian.

Jean-Christophe Penet lectured at the Université Lille 3 Charles-de-Gaulle (France), Dublin City University (Ireland) and the University of the West of England, Bristol before joining Newcastle University's School of Modern Languages as a Lecturer in French and Translation Studies in September 2010. His teaching at Newcastle University has led him to explore innovative uses of new technologies to enhance his students' motivation for language learning. He is a Fellow of the Higher Education Academy.

Christine Penman is a Senior Lecturer at Edinburgh Napier University. Educated in both France and the UK, she held a number of lecturing and research positions at the University of Stirling and worked as a freelance editor/lexicographer before joining Edinburgh Napier University in 2005. She currently coordinates the delivery of French modules and lectures on the cultural aspects of advertising on two post-graduate programmes. She has also been a Teaching Fellow since 2009 which reflects her interest in pedagogical issues. The focus of her academic research and publications has been on applied linguistics and on cultural and cross-cultural aspects of consumerism.

Debora Quattrocchi is an Associate Lecturer in the Faculty of Languages and Education, at the Open University in London, where she teaches Italian language and 'Exploring Languages and Cultures', an introductory module on intercultural communication. She has a first class degree in Modern Languages and Literature (Catania University, Italy), a BA Hons in English (Birkbeck, University of London) and an MRes in English Literature (Middlesex University). She is interested in issues relating to language learning and learning differences, language and identity and bilingualism and emotions.

Notes on contributors

Ania Rolińska is an EFL/EAP tutor and TELT Officer at School of Modern Languages at University of Glasgow. She is also an IELTS examiner, online teacher trainer (International House Online Teacher Trainer Institute) and a student (MSc in Digital Education at University of Edinburgh). She is a keen advocate of innovation and creativity in ELT and professional development. Her research interests include learner's autonomy, online course/activity design, multimodal approaches to writing and opportunities learning technologies offer for stimulating creativity and 'will to learn'.

Fernando Rosell-Aguilar is a lecturer in Spanish and an Open Media Fellow at the Open University, United Kingdom. His research focuses on online language learning, mainly podcasting and mobile apps as teaching and learning tools, CMC learning environments (such as audio and video conferencing) and digital literacy.

Stavroula Sokoli, PhD, is a researcher on Audiovisual Translation and Language Learning with over 20 publications in the area. She has initiated and coordinated the EU-funded projects "Learning via Subtitling" (http://levis.cti.gr) and ClipFlair (www.clipflair.net). She also collaborates with the Academic and Research Excellence Initiative in Greece (http://excellence.minedu.gov.gr). She teaches Spanish at the Hellenic Open University and as well as subtitling at the Universitat Pompeu Fabra and the Universitat Autònoma de Barcelona.

Sascha Stollhans holds a BA in German Linguistics and French Studies and an MA in German as a Foreign Language (Berlin). He has taught German at universities and language schools in Germany, France, South Africa and the UK, and is currently a DAAD-Lektor (language teacher appointed via the German Academic Exchange Service) and doctoral student at the University of Nottingham. His main teaching and research interests are contrastive linguistics, student engagement and learner autonomy, focus on form and collaborative dialogue, technology enhanced language learning (and its potential benefits on oral language skills) and content and language integrated learning (CLIL).

Notes on contributors

Juliet Vine spent several years teaching in China, before taking an MA in Translation. She is now a lecturer in the Department of Modern Languages and Culture, University of Westminster. She teaches Chinese to English translation and translation theory. Her research interests are related to translator training and translation quality assessment.

Shaoqun Wu is a Research Fellow in the Computer Science Department at the University of Waikato in New Zealand, and is the main developer of the FLAX language project. Her research interests include Computer Assisted Language Learning, Mobile Language Learning, Supporting Language Learning in MOOCs, Digital Libraries, Natural Language Processing and Computer Science education.

Aiden Yeh is an Assistant Professor at Wenzao Ursuline University of Languages where she teaches creative writing and other ESP courses (Research Writing, Mass Media, and Cross-Cultural Communications). She received her PhD in Applied Linguistics from the University of Birmingham, UK, and Master's in ELT Management from University of Surrey, UK.

Acknowledgements

This book would not have been possible without the support and enthusiasm of the dynamic and inspiring LLAS community working across the UK, Europe and the world. We thank them for their continued support of the LLAS elearning symposium, their enthusiasm for innovation and their boundless willingness to share their work and ideas with others.

We thank all of the authors who have contributed to this edited collection and who have shared their personal elearning journeys with us. We also thank the following people for their support during the creation of this book:

- Sylvie Thouësny at Research-publishing.net, for tireless support and advice through the publication process;

- Anna Comas-Quinn (Open University, UK) for her advice when the book was at the planning stage, and this volume owes much in its format and structure to a 2013 publication she co-edited[1];

- The team at the Centre for Languages, Linguistics and Area Studies www.llas.ac.uk.

Kate Borthwick, Erika Corradini and Alison Dickens

---

1. Beaven, A., Comas-Quinn, A., & Sawhill, B. (Eds). (2013). Case studies in openness in the language classroom. Dublin: Research-publishing.net. http://research-publishing.net/publications/2013-beaven-comas-quinn-sawhill/

Foreword

'Why, sometimes I've believed as many as six impossible things before breakfast'.
The White Queen talking to Alice in *Through the Looking Glass*.

I have been privileged to have attended all 10 LLAS elearning symposia and looking back over the last ten years, many of the everyday technological tools that are now pervasive in our daily lives would have seemed 'impossible' in 2005, the year of our first symposium. For example, Facebook, with over a billion users worldwide in 2014 was only founded the year before, in 2004. Google which now processes over 3.5 billion searches a day went public the same year. The first iPhone was launched in 2007, Twitter, the same year. WhatsApp, the messaging service, was only launched in 2009 and now has half a billion monthly users.

And yet despite this period of immense change in the way we use and access technology, we can see many common threads running through our symposia over these ten years. In 2005, one of our keynote speakers, Professor Gráinne Conole, asked us to consider the gap between the potential that new technologies offer us and reality, as well as the application of good pedagogical principles. We have continued to debate this theme regularly and no doubt will continue to do so.

Also in 2005, we were discussing how we can more effectively share the electronic resources we create for our learners and the benefits and barriers involved. As part of this discussion we felt that there was a need for new communities of practice in order to bring together those with pedagogical skills and those with technological skills. During the last ten years, we have developed these themes further, we have explored new ways of teaching and learning using technology, we have shared findings from the research we have carried out, meeting at the annual elearning symposium to exchange ideas.

The publication of this edited collection of work now celebrates precisely that community of practice that has developed over these years and the concept of

Foreword

sharing and open access. May I say thank you to all those who have participated in our elearning symposia in the past and who are now part of the community, and also welcome to all the readers of this volume and future participants in our next elearning symposia.

Let's continue to believe the impossible for our learners.

Professor Vicky Wright
Deputy Director of the Centre for Languages,
Linguistics and Area Studies (LLAS)

10 years of the LLAS elearning symposium: An introduction

Kate Borthwick[1], Erika Corradini[2], and Alison Dickens[3]

Welcome to this LLAS edited collection. This book is a celebration of and reflection on 10 years of the LLAS elearning symposium, an event which is run by the Centre for Languages, Linguistics and Area Studies based at the University of Southampton, UK.

1. What is LLAS?

The Centre for Languages, Linguistics and Area Studies (LLAS) was founded in 2000 as one of 24 Higher Education Academy[4] subject centres. Over time it has built a reputation for providing support to the wider languages, linguistics and area studies communities through its regular conferences, workshops and innovative projects which provide professional development and networking opportunities to teachers in the higher education and school sectors. More recently it has also become a successful enterprise unit within Modern Languages at the University of Southampton, which works in partnership with universities around the world to deliver bespoke professional development courses or develop collaborative projects.

---

1. University of Southampton, United Kingdom; k.borthwick@soton.ac.uk.

2. University of Southampton, United Kingdom; e.corradini@soton.ac.uk.

3. University of Southampton, United Kingdom; a.m.dickens@soton.ac.uk.

4. www.heacademy.ac.uk

How to cite this chapter: Borthwick, K., Corradini, E., & Dickens, A. (2015). 10 years of the LLAS elearning symposium: An introduction. In K. Borthwick, E. Corradini, & A. Dickens (Eds), *10 years of the LLAS elearning symposium: Case studies in good practice* (pp. 1-7). Dublin: Research-publishing.net. doi:10.14705/rpnet.2015.000262

Introduction

2. The LLAS elearning symposium

From rather modest beginnings this annual event has grown and been shaped by the wide and changing landscape of digital technologies. It began life in 2005 as a one-day event at which invited expert presenters gave us insights into topics such as mobile learning, re-useable learning objects and e-tutoring, much of which was new to us and probably to many others in the audience. It is now a two-day event, packed with presentations, workshops, technical showcases, poster sessions, and live-streamed keynote talks. It also has a virtual presence through Twitter[1], scoop.it[2] and the LLAS website[3].

It was at our first event that many of us first heard about web 2.0 from Professor (now Dame) Wendy Hall from the University of Southampton. Although this concept had been around for some time it had only just started to become widely used and the types of tools to which it referred were by no means as ubiquitous as they are today and certainly not routinely used in teaching. Moving through its subsequent 10 years the symposium has evolved to include a much wider range of experts, including those language teachers who initially formed the audience at the symposium, but who have subsequently showcased the many ways in which elearning tools and resources have been built into their own teaching. This reflects a key aim for the symposium that the main focus should be on the pedagogic benefits of incorporating technologies into course and learning design rather than on the tools themselves. Although, it is clear that the increasing range of tools and resources available to us and our students does play a significant role in the development of innovative, authentic and relevant teaching and learning practice.

Thus, our event has evolved from a forum at which elearning novices came to learn from the 'technology experts', such as Dame Wendy Hall and the many others who have been keynote presenters at the symposium over the years, to

---

1. @elearnllas #elearnllas

2. http://www.scoop.it/t/e-learning-symposium

3. www.llas.ac.uk

a meeting space for 'subject practitioner experts' to meet each other and share their practice. And this, in our view, has been a major contributor to the success of the symposium and to its longevity.

3. Content

In this volume, we hear from colleagues who have engaged with the symposium over the years, many of whom initially attended the event to learn from the experts and who have over the years metamorphosed into those very experts from whom others come to learn. They reflect on and celebrate this transformative dimension of the symposium in the case studies and personal reflections included in this edited collection.

This edited collection is structured around four sections. Each section begins with an invited contribution and contains articles related to the broad thematic area introduced in the invited piece. This structure deliberately reflects the alternation of keynote plenary sessions and talks which has been the distinct format of the elearning symposium in the past ten years. The book is aimed at practitioners and as such recounts real, practical experiences of innovation in using technology in language teaching or professional practice. The authors' work is based in research, but they all present lived examples of excellent practice in action. The range of projects and case studies presented in this volume is a testament to the irrepressible creativity of language teachers in their adoption of technology to achieve their pedagogic aims.

Over the past ten years, the symposium has followed the innovations brought about in the digital realm and has offered a yearly forum where technology and education have met. As some of the invited pieces show, the journey of technology in education has been a long and exciting one. Along the way, as all the contributions suggest, the symposium has brought innovative practice to the attention of teachers and learners and, perhaps more significantly for the connected world in which we operate, it has been a catalyst for the formation of an enthusiastic community – as this editorial project clearly shows.

Introduction

Marion Sadoux's personal journey with technology opens up Section 1. *Language learning in new contexts: mobile learning*. Starting from a language centre in the 1980s, she takes us from the clumsy physicality of audio cassettes right into the future, when as director of the Language Centre at University of Nottingham Ningbo (China), she tells us about her work with new digital communities in what is, as yet, a little known educational landscape. This section also features two case studies. Billy Brick's and Tiziana Cervi-Wilson's piece is centred on how in recent years the use of mobile technology for learning languages has gone beyond classroom walls. This study shows that it is now common practice among learners to use mobile devices for learning, and that devices or software which integrate traditional resources into mobile learning are in great demand. Fernando Rosell-Aguilar takes the key issues of mobile learning into the specific area of podcasting. By describing the innovations podcasting for language learning and teaching has undergone in the past ten years, Rosell-Aguilar's chapter brings to the reader's attention new ways of using podcasts when learning a language with suggestions about new formats and new practices.

Section 2. *Collaboration and open learning* is introduced by an expert in the field, Marina Orsini-Jones, from Coventry University. Through her ongoing commitment to technology-enhanced teaching and learning, Orsini-Jones takes us from CALL in its initial stages through to her latest project/s in telecollaboration for language learning. Her chapter explains the pedagogic principles underpinning her work and describes how technology can support the development of intercultural competence. Teresa Mackinnon's piece complements Orsini-Jones's article by describing the design of a large-scale blended learning environment for the Institution-Wide Language Programme (IWLP) at the University of Warwick. The aim of this project is twofold: to offer support to teachers in elearning and to allow them to network more effectively in a concerted effort to bring together 'participatory communities'. Jean-Christophe Penet explains how e-portfolios can be used as social media tools for language learners and for incorporating peer-learning into the broader area of elearning and virtual collaboration. Tita Beaven, meanwhile, focuses on the (re-)use of OER (Open Education Resources) by offering examples of how language teachers have unlocked the pedagogic potential of openly shared resources and adapted them to their own teaching needs and contexts. Anna Motzo and Debora Quattrocchi show how the open practices outlined in Beaven's chapter have been used in a project which features the collaborative design of OER for dyslexic learners of languages. Learning with dyslexia is a new area of pedagogic interest which deserves the attention of language teachers, as the authors suggest.

Julie Watson's piece opens Section 3. *Fostering creativity in the classroom*. Learning design is the focus of her piece and an area that Watson has developed through many projects involving the creation of online resources, courses and tools. The impact of her work is immediately visible in the first case study of this section in which Christine Penman explains how she put into practice Watson's work in the area of creating learning objects through using the LOC software. In particular, Penman describes the creative process underpinning the production of a series of resources centred on the combined study of language and literature. Ania Rolińska offers an example of learning technology at its most creative. Working with international students, she facilitated a project aimed at the production of visual artefacts resulting from the students' engagement with digital literacy and hypermedia. Edith Kreutner brings creativity to the teaching of grammar, an area often perceived as unexciting. Kreutner explains how movie making applied to grammar learning has engaged learners and empowered them throughout the learning process. This is an innovative project in an area that is currently experiencing revived interest and excitement. The final two case studies in this section relate technology and language learning to real-life scenarios. Aidan Yeh gives an account of a project carried out in a private university in Taiwan in the area of business English. The project's focus is to use technology to simulate real-life business situations for language learning. In a similar way to Yeh's, Juliet Vine's closing case study shows that the complexity of teaching translation can be addressed through using Wikis in ways which replicate real professional scenarios. Both of these projects offer students transferable, employability skills alongside their language skills.

Section 4. *New tools, new practices* begins with Benoît Guilbaud writing about connected learning and networked communities of practitioners. This article narrates Guilbaud's personal experience as a tutor and suggests that teaching practices are increasingly defined by the use of technology, whether collaborative tools or new engaging platforms and/or software. Sascha Stollhans, for example, introduces us to the use of Voxopop for learning German. Voxopop is a new platform which allows users to engage in discussions and exchange of ideas orally rather than in writing. This innovative aspect is, Stollhans suggests, beneficial to learners as they can record themselves and learn by listening in a friendly and easily accessible way. Learning through the production of audio books is the focus of Susana Lorenzo-Zamorano's chapter. Her piece reports the outcomes of a student-centred project which brought the use of tablet technology to the pedagogy of language, Spanish in this particular case. Rocío Baños and Stavroula Sokoli describe how the ClipFlair project inspired and motivated learners through re-voicing and captioning activities, now collected as resources in an easily accessible repository featuring 350 resources covering 15 different languages. Alannah Fitzgerald, Shaoqun Wu and María José Marín close this section with a chapter describing their innovative work with open access collections of corpus-based materials. They present a new, open source tool (FLAX) and show how a project working with English-language students has led to the adoption of open educational practices by teachers, and enabled students to take greater control and ownership over their own language learning.

4. And finally... thank you!

We hope that the case studies and personal learning journeys recounted here will be interesting and inspiring to you. They depict aspects of the development of technology-use in language teaching over the last ten years from the personal perspectives of people 'at the coalface' of teaching and learning. They also provide a snapshot of current good practice in using technology for teaching.

It has been a pleasure for us to read and collect the pieces together for this book. We have learnt much from them, and we learn new ideas and approaches each year that we run the symposium. We would like to thank everyone who has contributed to the elearning symposium itself, as participant, practice sharer, keynote presenter, workshop facilitator, online viewer, sponsor or as part of the organisation team. Technological innovation moves so fast that, like this book, each symposium only ever provides a snapshot in time, but we hope that the elearning symposium will continue to offer 'snapshots' for many more years to come.

Section 1.

Language learning in new contexts: Mobile learning

1 A journey to the East?
Trials and tribulations of a personal journey with technology and languages

Marion Sadoux[1]

---

1. How did you become interested in using technology in your professional life?

I started teaching languages in an Institution Wide Language Programme (IWLP) at the beginning of the 1990's. I had only ever used a word processor once; I had successfully used my parent's Minitel in France on a handful of operations. In my work, the use I make of technology for teaching, learning and leading programmes is always the by-product of a need or an idea for an intervention that has its roots elsewhere in the niggling gaps in my practice. In other words, technology is secondary to other considerations. The question of affordances is the only one that matters to me: it is not 'what can this tool do?', but 'what do I want to do, what can help me do it and help my students learn it?'

Back to the beginning: in those days, my university classrooms had no equipment other than a white or black-board to write on. Some more sophisticated classrooms were equipped with a retro-projector and I soon learnt how to make sure to book one of those. In the teachers' staff room, the photocopier was a hub of intense activity and conversations. To support our language teaching, we borrowed tape recorders, copies of the cassettes accompanying our dedicated textbooks, transparent slides for writing or photocopying purposes, fine permanent marker pens and thick whiteboard

---

1. University of Nottingham Ningbo, China; Marion.sadoux@nottingham.edu.cn.

How to cite this chapter: Sadoux, M. (2015). A journey to the East? Trials and tribulations of a personal journey with technology and languages. In K. Borthwick, E. Corradini, & A. Dickens (Eds), *10 years of the LLAS elearning symposium: Case studies in good practice* (pp. 11-19). Dublin: Research-publishing.net. doi:10.14705/rpnet.2015.000263

markers, all from a small technician's office located at the back of the Self Access Centre (SAC).

In sharp contrast with the teachers' staffroom, the SAC was full of technology: it had computers with sound cards, headphones and microphones, dedicated language learning software, CDs, DVDs and books. We were instructed to write a week-by-week self-study programme to accompany our taught courses. In the template that had been provided, the teachers had to designate the resources and activities that were to be used by students in the SAC. Some of the software available in the SAC contained authoring tools and in the first year, teachers had to use those to create multiple choice grammar exercises, gap-filling exercises to match the grammar points of their courses. These exercises were text based only and each input sentence or option choices were limited to a small number of typed characters.

Three images remain from those days. The first is that of colleagues and I stepping out of the Language Centre with great strain as we pushed the heavy wooden door to go to our classrooms dispersed on the university grounds, carrying our heavy daily attire of textbooks, cassettes, photocopies, cassette player, transparencies and pens. The second is the SAC we had to walk past would be full of diligent students in the first few weeks of teaching and then become gradually emptier as each day passed. The third is that of the blue screen of one of the Computer Assisted language Learning (CALL) programmes we had to use and the large flashing white cursor that would appear to let you input text. The sentiment that prevails when these images come back is one of powerlessness and frustration. Powerlessness, because there had been and would be no room for a long time for teachers to voice their thoughts or needs or what they perceived as their students' needs. The fact that students would gradually stop using the SAC or engaging with the self-study programme was not something that we could reflect upon or discuss –rather we were made to feel that this was our fault for not emphasising enough how important it was. Frustration, because some of us were keen to develop, craft, and design but had no say over the tools that we could use and no opportunity to appropriate others.

2. How has your use and knowledge of technology in language learning and teaching developed over time?

In the first few years of my career, I was repeatedly invited by my Director to contribute to the many CALL projects that the Language Centre was involved in. Inevitably, these would be projects that had been instigated by someone with technical knowledge and an ill-thought out notion of what would be good for language learners, and the teacher's role would be limited to providing the foreign language input. It was difficult to refuse and even more difficult to articulate reasons why one would not want to engage in this process. On the surface, this initial encounter with technology to enhance language teaching was a negative one. However, it is precisely in this apparent rejection of technology that lies the guiding principle of what has now become my core concern. Technology is neutral: what matters, is that it be driven by sound pedagogical concerns.

In many ways, my approach to technology in language teaching remains based on a *bricolage* ('Do it Yourself, DIY') approach –the tools may have changed but the methodology has not. Back then, I wanted to scaffold learning in class and used photocopied transparencies of the cartoons that came with the dialogues in the prescribed textbook in order to prepare students for listening and to ensure that they developed better listening skills that were not reliant on reading (with the textbook open) or on nothing at all (with the textbook closed). We would work from the images, play with the images, write over them with thought bubbles and produce relevant language and hypotheses around meaning before listening. I also used transparencies to write and project vocabulary on the board so that I would have a trace of the meanderings of my classes, one that I could re-use with exercises or compare with students notes. I call this *bricolage* because just as in DIY, it is about meeting a need promptly and being able to customise the end-product to very specific constraints. CALL was the bookcase you could buy already made from your local furniture store, but my walls were not even and I preferred to build my own shelving. Of course the tools do matter, but without knowing that the tools exist, one cannot envisage the solutions and sometimes one can remain blind to the problem.

3. How has contact with colleagues impacted on the way you use technology in language learning and teaching?

I was lucky in that my (reluctant) involvement in several CALL projects also earned me the opportunity to receive support from my university to attend workshops, seminars and conferences related to CALL. The first events of this kind that I attended were intimidating and, it seemed, driven by technology experts rather than ordinary language teachers. There were moments of inspiration though, such as a training session at the University of Hull, then home to the Tell consortium. There I received training in how to use an authoring package called *TransIt TIGER* (sadly no longer available but see Fayard, 1999). Although it was designed to support the teaching of translation, something which was not then part of my teaching area, this programme enabled tutors to upload a text, create hyperlinks to include definitions or translations and propose two or three different translations for students to compare. A vast improvement from the automated blank filling grammar exercises I had been accustomed to developing, this allowed for discourse level work to take place, and most importantly for work that did not result exclusively in a computer generating the right answer; there was space for critical thinking, for contrasting and comparing, for something which could be explored before a class and then extended into class activities. I promptly started using this software for other purposes, creating my own annotated texts with hyperlinks, working for the first time with distributive learning tools.

A few years later, the Internet having become more ubiquitous and available in a growing number of classrooms, I took a course in web–design on *Dreamweaver* and started developing my courses online. There was no virtual learning environment or learning management system in place (partly because our technicians were painstakingly trying to develop a languages specific one) and I started shaping my own teaching in a distributive way, empowering myself and my students to break the classroom walls, free our learning from time and place constraints and make better use of face-to-face sessions for oral interaction.

4. How do you use technology in your professional practice now?

The e-learning landscape has changed tremendously and for the better: communities of language teachers across the world collaborate, share and co-develop what has now become a much more accessible and pedagogically-grounded field of enquiry and practice. The processes and approaches through which I teach online or distribute teaching with digital tools have not changed much. My primary concern has remained one grounded in practice, reflection, identification of tools and evaluation of their affordances, design and testing. My practice however has shifted, as my career progressed to management and leadership roles, and my core interest now is in enabling others (language teachers and learners) to empower themselves to develop their use of technology for teaching and learning. This new direction has happened in the lifespan of the Centre for Languages Linguistics and Areas Studies (LLAS) and most particularly its annual e-Learning Symposium, which has been a constant source of learning, inspiration and support. A highly stimulating and engaging event, the symposium is an excellent opportunity to discover new tools and new approaches and to be reminded of the outstanding level of dynamism of the language teaching communities in terms of e-learning. For many who attend, communication and collaboration continues in between each symposium and weaves the threads of a dedicated community of practice.

One cannot underestimate the crucial role that can be played by such communities of practice in supporting language teachers to develop a personally meaningful and discipline relevant use of technology to support their teaching. Too often and for too many of us, the work we do in relation to technology is unseen, undervalued, ill-remunerated or accounted for, poorly supported and can be driven by external constraints rather than individual professional practice. When we receive training, this is often a dry show and tell which at best leaves us with a precarious sense of 'know how' and at worst generates high levels of anxiety and feelings of ineptitude. Rather than empowering teachers, it contributes to the de-professionalisation of the sector that has been noted in numerous instances and generates resistance and fear in relation to shifts in practice that are not only beneficial to enhancing the quality and achievements of our work, but are increasingly a must-do in the sector. From a management and leadership point-of-view, if one wants to do more than tick a box of compliance in a senior strategy document, e-learning is about change management and this is what most of my professional practice now involves.

5. How does your knowledge and experience in social media and web 2.0 technologies impact on your professional and teaching life?

The shift from pure classroom based teaching to the new distributed learning approaches that are recommended through most universities' teaching and learning agendas are a delicate affair which inevitably involve a radical and profound shift in one's position as teacher most notoriously coined by Alison King (1993) as a move from "sage on the stage" to "guide on the side" (p. 30). In other words, the empowerment that comes along with adopting technology to enhance teaching and learning necessitates a shift in authority through which the teacher relinquishes power to the learner.

My approach to scaffolding such a shift has been profoundly 'metalinguistic' in model as I have sought to develop practice through the establishment of a localised community of practice by making use of the very tools that I seek to empower my colleagues to explore and use. By creating internal virtual platforms for staff development and particularly for technology enhanced teaching, I have sought to offer colleagues an opportunity to develop a first person experience of what it can mean to learn online as well as face-to-face. In turn, staff development sessions have been set up on a distributive basis, where teachers have been able to scaffold their learning before a face-to-face session, during the session and beyond the session. Another important aspect of the way in which I try to approach my practice in terms of programme leadership, is that I try to maintain the focus on enabling –something which takes time and requires others to contribute– but I am also sharply aware of the necessity to address a number of disruptive constraints. First of all, working in an IWLP, I have to abide by university standards and guidelines –these are extremely variable, more or less constricting and more or less helpful. Some universities provide extensive support and structure to operate within; others are a little more vague. The years I spent at London Metropolitan University were extremely productive in developing leadership in technology enhanced learning and teaching. The Centre for the Enhancement of Learning and Teaching (CELT) has a vibrant e-learning section (Hamby, Pettiward, Lister, & Fregona, n.d.) led by lecturers who act as blended learning facilitators. There is both a cascade model of training and policy which works in a dialogical way: the blended learning facilitators receive dedicated training, it is matured into pedagogical practice, shared and further reflected upon to develop an openly constructed strategy at university level. This, in turn, supplied a useful template for learning, evolving and decision-making that could be reproduced and further enhanced at micro level. The university I work with now is a young institution, which is yet to effectively set up its e-learning support beyond the mere basics of technical training. Whether practice is dictated or negotiated makes an enormous difference on teaching staff and on the way in which they are able to approach adoption and development around technology.

Another area, which in my view remains problematic in all institutions, is the value that the institution is prepared to attach to e-learning in real terms. In other words, how much of our time do these institutions think we should reasonably devote to developing our practice in relation to technology? How can teachers, leaders, institutions be accountable for this time? Many universities brandish online-courses as a solution to economical challenges and an area where they can compete at lower costs –many also believe that teaching staff can be trained with two-hour demonstrations here and there. In reality, whether we seek to use digital tools to distribute learning across a wider range of platforms (face-to-face, independent and collaborative online) or to fully deploy our teaching expertise onto online realms, the time required to successfully engage with technology is enormous and goes well beyond the need for occasional training. Developing an online teaching presence (without which it is doubtful that learners will do more than lurk) does not merely require the creation and uploading of digitised materials, but also necessitates the considerations for instructional and navigational design, managing and monitoring of learner activity, ability (and time) to select the tool with the best affordances for the right task; the model of one hour's time to prepare each hour of teaching obviously bears no relation to what truly goes on here. Moreover, it would also be equally important for institutions to reflect and guide their staff better in relation to the invasiveness of technology: if learning on-the-go, anywhere, anytime may be desirable, does this mean that working on-the-go, anywhere, anytime should become the rule too? Technology can also infringe upon public and personal spaces: educators also need support to better understand the risks they may be running as they deploy their teaching through various social networking platforms (and in turn students need guidance on this too). The issue of time and recognition is an enormous problem and clearly one that threatens the development of practice beyond a few mavericks who are prepared to invest personally. The question of risk is one which needs to be addressed too if we want to progress from digital deviance to professionalism.

The last step on my journey takes me to China, working behind the great firewall with slow broadband connections, and beginning to understand very different constraints in relation to e-learning: the sharp difference here, between public and private (mostly anonymous or in elected closed circles) uses of technology, the correlated and multiple online identities that develop in such a context along with the differing genre of digital literacies and narratives but also the sheer complexities around establishing group work among students on or offline. Most of my preferred tools, metaphorically and practically do not work here, or, at best, not reliably. Having on occasions felt stripped of my tools, I am also developing a clear sense that much of the theory behind both e-learning and language teaching are intractably Western in assumptions. Neither seems to fully account for the needs of Chinese learners who probably need a different kind of scaffolding in order to develop a safe online cognitive presence as much as they require another panoply of tasks to engage in productive meaningful language activities in a classroom. The next step on this journey will be to work collaboratively with students and colleagues to investigate how their digital literacies and learning styles can be harnessed to design suitable learning pathways and navigational architectures for our module Moodle pages, work which I hope to share with colleagues at the forthcoming LLAS e-learning symposium.

References

Fayard, N. (1999). Integrating TransIt-TIGER French into the second year language curriculum. *CALL-EJ Online, 1*(1).

Hamby, L., Pettiward, J., Lister, P., & Fregona, C. (n.d.). *London met eLearning matrix* [website]. Retrieved from www.celtelearning.org

King, A. (1993). *From sage on the stage to guide on the side*. College Teaching, 41(1), 30-35. doi:10.1080/87567555.1993.9926781

2 Technological diversity: A case study into language learners' mobile technology use inside and outside the classroom

Billy Brick[1] and Tiziana Cervi-Wilson[2]

Abstract

The speed of technological advance in the mobile phone, netbook and tablet markets has meant that learners increasingly have access to digital devices capable of enhancing their learning experience. This case study reports on how language learners, taking Italian as an option on the Institution Wide Languages Programme (IWLP) at Coventry University, use their digital devices to support their language learning. Foreign language educators in higher education need to be aware of the degree to which learners utilise their digital devices and what they use them for. This knowledge will allow tutors to be able to offer help and support. Learners were observed using their devices in the classroom and were asked to complete a detailed questionnaire. More detailed data was then collected from a focus group of students reflecting on the numerous ways in which they used their phones to support their language learning. The case study found that the use of digital devices to support language learning was widespread and often took place outside the classroom. It also revealed that tutors were unable to recommend appropriate apps and that learners tended to use their devices autonomously and unintegrated with their modules. Learners expressed a desire for the integration of mobile language learning resources with their existing course books and on-line learning materials.

Keywords: MALL, Italian, digital devices, language learning, smartphones, apps.

---

1. Coventry University, Coventry, United Kingdom; lsx133@coventry.ac.uk.

2. Coventry University, Coventry, United Kingdom; lsx091@coventry.ac.uk.

How to cite this chapter: Brick, B., & Cervi-Wilson, T. (2015). Technological diversity: A case study into language learners' mobile technology use inside and outside the classroom. In K. Borthwick, E. Corradini, & A. Dickens (Eds), *10 years of the LLAS elearning symposium: Case studies in good practice* (pp. 21-30). Dublin: Research-publishing.net. doi:10.14705/rpnet.2015.000264

Chapter 2

1. Context/rationale

Digital devices have become increasingly indispensable artefacts in modern society and people's dependence on them has increased accordingly. More recently, the advent of smart phones, with the ability to connect to the internet, has added a number of additional computing capabilities to the basic function of telephony. Thanks to these new functions, smart phones have become powerful mobile learning devices, sharing many educational applications with computers. Furthermore, for reasons of convenience, mobile phones are even more effective than computers in the Web 2.0 context, allowing users to create, share and disseminate knowledge. In this context, pedagogical concerns have arisen regarding when and where it is appropriate to use mobile phones, not least within universities. Tutors may disagree on mobile device campus usage policy but most would agree that mobile devices have the potential to distract and disrupt.

There were two distinct contexts to the study: how learners utilise their digital devices inside the classroom in formal settings, and how they use them informally outside the classroom. This approach mirrors Kukulska-Hulmes's (2012) study which concluded that:

> "time and place are becoming more prominent in shaping the landscape of language learning as learning intertwines with their daily life activity and work. I have sought to look beyond the "anytime, anywhere" mantra to discover the specifics of time and place, enabling the formulation of some key questions and choices that can be used to interrogate and develop future designs for mobile language learning" (pp. 10-11).

At Coventry University, mobile phone usage in lectures is not permitted, but their role in the language classroom is more ambiguous due to the potential affordances they provide in language learning contexts. One of the main attractions for incorporating mobile phones in the classroom is that apps can be used in tandem within class curriculum in order to help students understand complex linguistic structures. In fact, one of the motivations for carrying out the study came from one of the researcher's continual observations of learners surreptitiously using their devices during class. This observation ignited a desire to capture more in depth data regarding digital device usage inside and outside the classroom. The researchers attempted to establish whether learners were utilising their devices as portable dictionaries or whether they exploited them in a more sophisticated way. In addition, data was collected regarding the specific use of their devices outside the classroom in autonomous settings.

One difficulty encountered by the researchers, which was also apparent during the classroom observations and in the focus group, concerned the definition of the term 'app'. During discussions with learners it became clear that they were not always aware if they were accessing their learning material via an app, or via either a smartphone-optimised website, or the original designed-for-PC or laptop website. Indeed, the distinctions between these can be subtle and not always immediately obvious. If the Guardian Newspaper is taken as an example, the complex nature of the way in which a website can be viewed can be further clarified (see Table 1).

Table 1. The various ways of viewing the Guardian Newspaper

Name of App	Specific Features	Availability Offline	Cost
Guardian and Observer iPad Edition	Specifically designed for use on the iPad. Requires iOS5	Yes	Subscription
The Guardian for iPhone and iPad	Specifically designed for use on the iPhone but will also work on the iPad 3	Yes	Free
Guardian Kindle Edition	Available for all Kindles	Yes	Subscription
Guardian Blackberry 10 App	Available for one specific Blackberry phone	Yes	Free
Guardian Android App	Free download for Android devices	Yes	Free
Guardian Mobile Site	Guardian main website optimized for use on mobile devices	Yes	Free
Guardian Windows App	App for use on Windows phones	Yes	Free

Table 1 serves to illustrate that questions focussing specifically on apps could have been slightly misconstrued or misunderstood by participants. Most major websites now have a plethora of mobile apps similar to the Guardian's, which may be confusing.

A recent study by Simon and Fell (2012) found that 60% of foreign language students used their smart phones for language learning purposes. Mobile devices are at the forefront of recent developments in language learning with a plethora of third party apps available from the two main companies: Android and Apple. A search for language learning apps on these online stores produces hundreds of results ranging from full language courses to tourist phrase books, dictionaries and flash cards (for a thorough explanation of the variety of apps available see Godwin-Jones, 2011). Many of these apps are free of charge and others cost up to 10 USD depending on their perceived value. Some companies give their apps away for free if the consumer has already subscribed to their online offer whilst others use the 'Freemium' model to sell their apps. This large choice of apps can be explained by a significant increase in demand for language learning from developing countries where learning a language can have significant impact on employment and trade (Kukulska-Hulme, 2012).

Yet few studies have investigated students' personal use of language learning mobile apps and the learning benefits students perceive they bring. Indeed most research into mobile learning in university settings has tended to focus on teacher-led mobile initiatives. Although there are apps for all aspects of language learning, very little consideration has been given to the pedagogical premises that underpin the design of mobile apps.

2. Aims and objectives

This case study involved a sample of 175 learners across three year groups. It captured detailed data regarding the devices owned, specific apps, as well as other features learners accessed in order to facilitate their learning. It also recorded learners' views regarding the support and advice they expected to receive from their tutors. The purpose of this research was to answer the question: 'how do language learners use their mobile devices to support their language learning?' More specifically, the research had three objectives:

- to establish the specific ways in which users use their digital devices inside and outside the classroom;

- to establish which specific sites and apps they access;

- to explore the ways in which learners would like to use their digital devices.

3. What we did

The participants in the project were 175 undergraduate learners, 68.1% were from the UK, 13.2% were from Romania and the rest were from various L1 backgrounds. All of the students were taking Italian at levels 1, 2 and 3 on the IWLP between October 2011 and April 2012. 71% of the participants were taking a beginners' level module. At Coventry University all IWLP provision is organised by the Department of English and Languages, and falls within a compulsory 10 credit employability scheme called Add+vantage Coventry University. The scheme, launched in October 2006, is unique and has greatly increased IWLP provision across the University. These students were studying a variety of different degree programmes across the University.

In the first part of the study, learners were observed using their digital devices in the classroom and were asked to explain how they were using them to support their language learning. They were also asked to complete a three-part, online questionnaire which was administered in class. Most of the learners already had some experience of language learning technologies incorporated in university-style learning and teaching. The first section asked learners to indicate the devices they owned and to state how, when and where they used them. The second section then aimed to gain an understanding of the frequency with which they used their devices. Learners had to rate questions on a five-point Likert scale, in order to capture data referring to specific usage of their devices in the four skills of reading, writing, speaking and listening. Finally, learners were invited to explain how they used their devices to access dictionaries, translation-sites, thesauruses and other Italian language learning sites. To triangulate the study, semi-structured interviews were carried out with a sample of the participants, in which more detailed questions were posed. Both researchers were always present as a means of cross-checking and producing a more complete record. Of the 175 participants who completed the online survey, 10 took part in the focus groups. The distribution of gender was skewed towards females, with 61% females, and 39% males. Because all of the participants were studying on the University-wide languages programme, only 20% were studying languages as their main degree; the vast majority (80%) were not specialist language learners. The interviews were semi-structured and took place over a period of two weeks following the completion of the questionnaires.

The following section is a summary of the questionnaires and evaluations collected from the participants both in the classroom and via classroom observations. The combination of regular dialogue and discussion with the students, and questionnaire data and focus group observations, provided a diverse variety of data covering a wide range of opinions about their usage of their devices.

4. Discussion

Learners at all levels were surveyed, but as is the case on all IWLPs, the overwhelming majority (62%) were learning Italian at beginners level. However, there was no evidence to suggest that this affected the overall outcome of the research. 78% of our sample stated that they owned a digital device and of these, 69% owned either an Apple, Blackberry or HTC device. In terms of operating systems, they were equally divided between Apple, Android and Research in Motion (RIM).

Just over 22.3% of respondents stated that they used their digital devices to access online dictionaries with the most popular being WordReference. However, many chose not to use a dictionary at all and instead opted for online translators, overwhelmingly Google Translate. The respondents who took part in the focus group stated unanimously that they would like advice from their tutors regarding which online dictionary was most suitable for learners at their level. This is not surprising given the large number of free-to-use electronic dictionaries available. However, perhaps it is unrealistic to expect tutors to have the time or expertise to recommend specific dictionaries. This is particularly apposite in Coventry University's context where language learning modules are taught two hours per week over ten weeks and two of these weeks are dedicated to assessment. In this context, tuition in dictionary use is not a high priority. In spite of this, there was a clear desire from the focus group and from individuals during the classroom observations for tutors to be aware of the various language specific apps so that they can offer appropriate advice to learners.

Only 17% either agreed or strongly agreed that they used their devices to practice their listening skills whilst the figure for writing was 20%. In the focus group, several respondents stated that they downloaded the mp3 files associated with their course book onto their digital devices and this was actively encouraged by their tutor. The researchers did not establish whether those who responded positively to the writing question, wrote on their phones, tablets or on laptops. Some of the focus group participants mentioned screen size as a factor which discouraged them from writing on their digital devices.

Learners were also asked whether or not they used their devices to look up the meanings and spellings of words. The question did not seek to ascertain whether they used bilingual dictionaries, multilingual dictionaries or online translation programmes such as Google Translate. 64% either agreed or strongly agreed whilst 30% stated that they disagreed or strongly disagreed with the statement. This is clear evidence that a large proportion of learners are using their digital devices to find out the meaning of words. Observations in the classroom demonstrate that learners are choosing to use their devices for looking up the meanings of words rather than using traditional paper dictionaries.

Only 53% of the participants either agreed or strongly agreed that they took full advantage of digital technologies to support their language learning. This suggests that there is considerable scope to teach learners the ways in which they could integrate their mobile devices into their language learning.

The important issue concerning the responsibility of tutors in the age of Web 2.0 was highlighted by Conole and Alevizou (2010) who wrote that "the boundaries between traditional roles (teacher and learner) and functions (teaching and learning) are blurring. 'Teachers' need to be learners in order to make sense of and take account of new technologies in their practices" (p. 44). However, the fast changing nature of technology and increasing pressures on staff time may be obstacles to staff development and training in these areas.

Furthermore, 58% of learners used an online dictionary or translator. When asked to specify the name of their favoured translator, nearly 82% stated that they used Google Translate. Participants in the focus group suggested that Google Translate was used in a similar way to a dictionary: to find out the meanings of individual words. Interestingly, the majority of the focus group participants were unable to make a distinction between an online translator and an online dictionary. This is perhaps understandable given that 80% of the participants were not language specialists.

The revelation that learners relied on the rating system used on Apple, Android and Blackberry app sites rather than advice from tutors, suggests that there is some scope for teacher training in this area. There are very few practitioners' websites available where language learning apps are categorised and evaluated with the notable exception of The University of Colorado Boulder, where both free and paid-for multi-language and language specific apps are recommended along with other language learning resources.

Participants in the focus group voiced a strong desire to have a dedicated app for their language learning module which synced with their virtual learning environment, but this sort of integrated approach across printed and digital resources is still some way from being realised.

5. Conclusion

In this case study, it has been argued that participants are using their smart phones and digital devices in a wide range of contexts to support their language learning both inside and outside the classroom.

Ongoing technological change will continue to be a challenge to researchers as innovation in the phone market shows no sign of abating. This may offer new possibilities and open new avenues for researchers in this field. Educational practitioners will have to continue developing frameworks to optimise mobile learning and their efforts will continue to be challenged by technological change.

The study highlights the need for practitioners to be aware of the ever-changing technological landscape so that they are able to recommend suitable technologies to optimise the use of technology in language learning. It is difficult to see how mobile-assisted language learning can avoid the pitfalls that have affected CALL, namely that research has tended to follow technological innovations rather than vice versa. Our study clearly shows that practitioners need to be actively involved in the affordances offered by mobile devices, if they wish to be able to offer up-to-date advice to their learners. One of the key points highlighted throughout our study is the extent to which learners are using their mobile devices without concomitant support offered by practitioners. Hence, suitable resources need to be made available to equip practitioners with the necessary skills to offer advice to enhance students' language learning experience in the mobile environment. Another approach, which also addresses the digital literacy agenda, would be to engage learners in evaluation tasks, such as evaluating the affordances of websites and apps or rating such sites themselves.

References

Conole, G., & Alevizou, P. (2010). *A literature review of the use of Web 2.0 tools in higher education*. Higher Education Academy. Retrieved from https://www.heacademy.ac.uk/sites/default/files/Conole_Alevizou_2010.pdf

Godwin-Jones, R. (2011). *Emerging technologies. Mobile Apps for Language Learning. Language Learning & Technology, 15*(2), 2-11. Retrieved from http://llt.msu.edu/issues/june2011/emerging.pdf

Kukulska-Hulme, A. (2012). Language learning defined by time and place: A framework for next generation designs. In J. E. Díaz-Vera (Ed.), *Left to My Own Devices: Learner Autonomy and Mobile Assisted Language Learning. Innovation and Leadership in English Language Teaching, 6* (pp. 1-13). Bingley, UK: Emerald Group Publishing Limited. Retrieved from http://oro.open.ac.uk/30756/1/AKH_Emerald_chapter_FINAL.pdf

Simon, E. F., & Fell, C. P. (2012, June 6). Using mobile learning resources in foreign language instruction. *Educause Review Online*. Retrieved from http://www.educause.edu/ero/article/using-mobile-learning-resources-foreign-language-instruction

3 Podcasting as a language teaching and learning tool

Fernando Rosell-Aguilar[1]

Abstract

This paper looks back at the last 10 years of the use of podcasting as a language teaching and learning tool. It considers the potential that was identified at the early stages, to the work that has been carried out to evaluate whether this potential has actually been realised. It presents a taxonomy of podcasts that can be used for language learning and suggestions regarding the format of podcasts. It also reports on how users utilise podcasts and on how different audiences have markedly different practices. It concludes that podcasting allows learners flexibility and personalised learning.

Keywords: podcasting, language learning, OER, iTunes, users, evaluation, eLearning, mobile learning.

1. Context/rationale

Podcasting technology became popular around 2004-2005 and in 2005 'podcast' was named 'word of the year' by the editors of the Oxford American Dictionary (BBC News, 2005). Since then, podcasting technology has spread, expanded what it can do and become easier to use. This has led to its adoption by individuals, businesses, the arts, the media and, of course, education.

I became interested in podcasting in 2005, after experiencing as a learner how practical having my own teaching resources (audio and video files) on my

---

1. The Open University, United Kingdom; Fernando.rosell-aguilar@open.ac.uk.

How to cite this chapter: Rosell-Aguilar, F. (2015). Podcasting as a language teaching and learning tool. In K. Borthwick, E. Corradini, & A. Dickens (Eds), *10 years of the LLAS elearning symposium: Case studies in good practice* (pp. 31-39). Dublin: Research-publishing.net. doi:10.14705/rpnet.2015.000265

iPod was. As a researcher, I produced a taxonomy of podcasts for language learning based on whether the podcasts were conceived as a language learning resource or not (Rosell-Aguilar, 2007). Podcasts that can benefit language learners include those that teachers and students develop as a language learning activity, and the use of 'authentic' existing, audio resources. These may be language learning courses which use podcasts (either at the core of their teaching or as supplementary materials) or the vast amount of authentic materials available online, from news items to programmes about any subject in the target language.

When podcasting became popular, researchers became interested in how it could be used for educational purposes (see Rosell-Aguilar, 2007 for a review of the literature in this area). They quickly identified that podcasting was a convenient and easy to use format. They hypothesised that it would be attractive or 'cool' for students, and also motivating. They pointed out that the technology made podcasts easy to access, and that for educational providers it would be good value for money, as podcasts are relatively cheap to produce, and it would give those institutions that provided them good publicity and face value, as they would be seen as using the latest technology. The other big advantage identified was portability: the idea that you could access learning anytime and anywhere.

Podcasting fits with the current movement towards free open-access educational content, as exemplified by Open Educational Resources (OERs) and Massive Open Online Courses (MOOCs). These are alternatives to formal study, although they can be combined with it, and bring learning to people who might otherwise not have access to it. Learners do not usually follow a traditional pathway through these, but instead choose what is of interest to them personally.

A subject that was identified early on as one that would clearly benefit from the availability of audio and video resources made available online was modern languages: language teachers had been using audio cassettes, CDs and videos for a long time before podcasting came along. Those audiovisual materials, however, had to be purchased or borrowed from a library, and their availability was limited. Their audience was people who were interested in learning and made the effort to seek those resources and pay for them. With podcasts, materials became free and easy to find, and also easy to play without the need for language laboratories or multiple devices. Within seconds you could have it in your mp3 player, mobile phone or many other devices (the list has grown immensely and rapidly in the last ten years). In 2007, I proposed a taxonomy of language learning podcasts, presented in Figure 1.

Figure 1. Taxonomy of uses of podcasting for language learning (adapted from Rosell-Aguilar, 2007, p. 476)

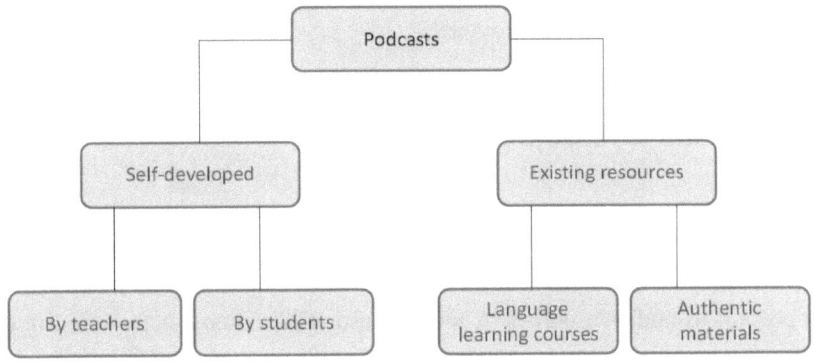

Language learning podcasts vary enormously in terms of design format: long monologues, bite-sized information, interactive conversations, vocabulary lists, phrase of the day, recipes, interviews, news, showcases of student work, etc. They also vary in terms of quality. Like any other resource (videos, CDs, websites) some will appeal to some types of students and others will appeal to other types. In 2007 I suggested that language learning course podcasts should:

- provide exposure to the language and its characteristics;

- use a range of materials, including authentic materials;

- provide explicit learning outcomes with clear objectives within a defined syllabus;

- provide exposure to the culture of the areas where the target language is spoken;

- be engaging and of adequate length;

- have a clear consideration of the medium: including portability and screen size (Rosell-Aguilar, 2007, p. 489).

It would be unlikely for a podcast to do all these, but the list provides a model that more and more podcasts now use.

2.   Aims and objectives

Research projects carried out with language learning podcasts have found positive attitudes from users as well as indications of improvement in certain skills, mainly those to do with the aural skills that are naturally better served by podcast as audio resources. A lot of questions remained unanswered in the research about podcast use, however: who downloads podcasts? What for? And how do they use them? Do they learn just as well, better or worse than with other materials?

Researchers started to look at what their students were actually doing with the podcasts and the results were somewhat different from what they had foreseen. They found that learners liked using iPods for learning and found them convenient and attractive, but there was no certainty about whether this was due to the novelty factor. The research also found that listening to educational podcasts was perceived as an academic activity, and that students who took part in the research were not transferring the mp3s to their mobile devices; instead they mostly listened at their computer (Lee & Chan, 2007; McKinney, Dyck, & Luber, 2009; O'Bannon, Lubke, Beard, & Britt, 2011). These findings cast doubt over some of the potential benefits that had been identified, such as the fact that listening to podcasts would not feel like studying or that podcasting enabled people to listen on the move. However, the research projects that found these results were largely carried out by teachers using their own groups of learners and distributing the podcasts through their university's Virtual Learning Environments (VLEs). Therefore, it was hardly surprising that students perceived the listening activity as an academic activity. Also, because the students who took part had to download the podcasts from their VLE on their computers, it made sense to listen at the same computer without transferring to a mobile device.

The issue was that the results gathered from this type of practice tended to be generalised to all types of podcasting, when in fact they applied only to the context of teachers providing their own students with podcasts.

3. What I did: the iTunesU research project

Without a doubt the largest channel for distribution of educational podcasts is the Apple Corporation's iTunesU. It was launched in 2007 as a method for US and Canadian universities to distribute content for their courses. Some of the content these universities uploaded to iTunesU was restricted to their own students, and some of it was made available to anyone who wanted to download and listen to it. Apple talked about its new service as a 'university in your pocket' and highlighted the unprecedented access to lectures and materials that were previously only available to a minority.

Apple soon invited universities from further afield to join iTunesU, and nowadays universities from many countries offer free materials for download. These include world renowned institutions such as Harvard, Yale, MIT, Stanford, Oxford, Cambridge, and La Sorbonne. As well as the materials from universities, iTunesU now also incorporates resources from other educational institutions, such as colleges and museums in a section called *Beyond Campus*.

Chapter 3

iTunesU has become incredibly successful, and it reached its billionth download in 2013. With iTunes podcasts, and iTunesU in particular, the context of learning is completely different to the research carried out beforehand. These resources are being consumed by the general public, people who are not following a formal learning pathway.

To find out more about the use of iTunesU for language learning, I set up a research study based on iTunesU at the UK's Open University (OU). As a distance learning provider, the OU has a 40-year history of delivering high-quality teaching content through different media. iTunesU at the OU was launched in 2008 and now it is one of the institutions that generates the most downloads on iTunesU; it reached 65 million in 2013, making it the largest provider of iTunesU materials in Europe. The three main questions I wanted to answer in my research study were: who downloads podcasts from iTunes U? What do they do with the podcasts? And what do they think of them? I created a survey and a link to it was placed on every iTunesU at the OU page, including its home page.

Over 2000 people took part in the study, of which 455 were language learners. About 60% of the respondents were between 25 and 54. This was surprising to me because previous research participants had been much younger. Only just over 1% of the respondents were under 15 and only about 6% were 15 to 18. People also tend to associate new technologies with men, and there were indeed more men than women among participants. It was not a large difference –56% men– but considering that there tends to be more women than men enrolled on university courses overall nowadays, it suggested that podcasting attracts more men than women. This may not be the case for much longer, however, because when gender and age were correlated, the data show that in the older age brackets there were more men than women, whereas among the younger users women outnumbered men. Another difference from the participants of previous research into podcasting use was that around 60% of the people who took part in the survey were employed, and fewer than 20% were students. In the previous studies reported in the research, the vast majority of participants were students.

The results of the research have been published in separate articles on different aspects of the project. One focused on all iTunesU learners (Rosell-Aguilar, 2013a) and another on language learners (Rosell-Aguilar, 2013b). Further work on the data also produced insights into mobile learning.

I asked participants why they were interested in the podcasts they downloaded. Only 17% said that it was because these podcasts were relevant to their current studies, around 11% listened because the podcasts were relevant to their profession, and the rest, over 70%, did it because of personal interest. This confirms that most people are part of the general public who are interested in learning without a specific purpose such as work or formal studies. I also asked if the podcasts were the main source of learning for the subject they had an interest in. Whereas only 10% of non-language learners used podcasts as their main method of learning, this doubled to 20% in the case of language learners.

When it comes to what they did with the podcasts, over half of the people who responded to the survey listened on a portable device: their mp3 player or their phone. When asked if listening to the podcasts was something they do as an activity they set time aside for, or if it was something they do as part of another activity, around 55% of non-language learners said they listen whilst doing something else, such as commuting or exercising, whereas for language learners this figure went up to almost 63%. The participants rated the quality of the podcasts very highly, and over 97% said that the podcasts are helping them learn about the subjects they are interested in.

4.   Discussion

The results of my research showed a picture of the podcast user and their opinions that is very different from previous research. It suggests the differences in practices have a lot to do with context: where users find these podcasts and why they are listening (whether as formal learners, e.g. a student who is doing homework, or as informal learners). It also shows that for most people listening

Chapter 3

to podcasts is not an academic activity and that podcasting can be considered a mobile technology after all; the university really is in your pocket.

It is very interesting that language learners were twice as likely to use podcasts as the main source of learning, and more likely to listening 'on the go' whilst doing other activities. It suggests that language learning is perceived by some as something that can be learnt by informal listening only, rather than through formal learning.

It is true that these results are from only one university, but considering the vast majority of respondents were not actually Open University students, it is fairly safe to assume that this profile probably fits many users of iTunesU resources from other universities as well. Since most respondents in my research were not enrolled on any courses, just curious to learn, it probably does not matter to them which university they download podcasts from. They just pick and choose what is of interest, in a similar manner to the way people use OERs or MOOCs. Different resources will appeal to different learners, or to the same learners depending on their mood, location, or preference.

5. Conclusion

The high rating of podcasting as a learning tool is a fantastic response and it means that what universities are doing, putting their materials out there for people to find, is very worthwhile. iTunesU has brought a richness of freely available material that simply was not available to the general public before. It is an enormous public library that can deliver resources straight to your device and into your ears, only you do not have to return the materials afterwards. People do not have to register or pay fees, they do not have time pressures to complete studies by a deadline, and they can pick and choose whatever they like.

The main benefit is that podcasting in general, and iTunesU in particular, allows people to learn whatever they are interested in at their own pace, where they like, when they like. It is personalised learning in a way that has never been achieved before. It is also bringing learning to all kinds of people from all over the world, who may otherwise be unable or unwilling to access formal education. As an educator, I think that is a great development, and something that everyone involved should be proud of.

References

BBC News. (2005, December 7). *Wordsmiths hail podcast success*. Retrieved from http://news.bbc.co.uk/1/hi/technology/4504256.stm

Lee, M. J. W., & Chan, A. (2007). Pervasive, lifestyle-integrated mobile learning for distance learners: An analysis and unexpected results from a podcasting study. *Open Learning: The Journal of Open, Distance and e-Learning, 22*(3), 201-218.

McKinney, D., Dyck, J. L., & Luber, E. S. (2009). iTunes university and the classroom: Can podcasts replace professors? *Computers & Education, 52*(3), 617-623. doi:10.1016/j.compedu.2008.11.004

O'Bannon, B. W., Lubke, J. K., Beard, J. L., & Britt, V. G. (2011). Using podcasts to replace lecture: Effects on student achievement. *Computers & Education, 57*(3), 1885-1892. doi:10.1016/j.compedu.2011.04.001

Rosell-Aguilar, F. (2007). Top of the pods–In search of a podcasting "Podagogy" for language learning. *Computer Assisted Language Learning, 20*(5), 471-492. doi:10.1080/09588220701746047

Rosell-Aguilar, F. (2013a). Delivering unprecedented access to learning through podcasting as OER, but who's listening? A profile of the external iTunes U user. *Computers & Education, 67*, 121-129. doi:10.1016/j.compedu.2013.03.008

Rosell-Aguilar, F. (2013b). Podcasting for language learning through iTunes U: The learner's view. *Language Learning & Technology, 17*(3), 74-93. Retrieved from http://llt.msu.edu/issues/october2013/rosellaguilar.pdf

Section 2.

Collaboration and open learning

4 A reflective e-learning journey from the dawn of CALL to web 2.0 intercultural communicative competence (ICC)

Marina Orsini-Jones[1]

---

1. How did you become interested in using technology in your professional life?

I graduated from the University of Bologna in Modern Foreign Languages and Literature in 1984 and I remember the painstaking job of typing my 40,000 word dissertation on American literature on an old Olivetti type-writer. Umberto Eco had just started publicising an innovation called the 'Word-processor', but unfortunately I did not know anything about it and the quality of the final version of my first dissertation (with visible Tippex marks) provides embarrassing evidence of this.

I obtained my first graduate job as Italian language assistant with the British Council and was 'sent to Coventry', to the then *Lanchester Polytechnic*, currently *Coventry University*, where the German and Russian teams were experimenting with what would probably be called 'blended learning' these days, with little BBC micros –black screen, white letters, state-of-the-art Computer Assisted Language Learning (CALL) back then– and there was evidence that their experiments were being well received by students. I found this encounter with CALL and the way technology could support both professional development and the learning journey of students very inspiring. It was thus that my interest in technology in education started.

---

1. Coventry University, United Kingdom. m.orsini@coventry.ac.uk.

How to cite this chapter: Orsini-Jones, M. (2015). A reflective e-learning journey from the dawn of CALL to web 2.0 intercultural communicative competence (ICC). In K. Borthwick, E. Corradini, & A. Dickens (Eds), *10 years of the LLAS elearning symposium: Case studies in good practice* (pp. 43-56). Dublin: Research-publishing.net. doi:10.14705/rpnet.2015.000266

2. How has your use and knowledge of technology in language learning and teaching developed over time?

The new generation of computers and software packages that became available in the early 1990s enabled me to better incorporate socio-cultural themes into language learning. For example, I co-created with my students *La neve nel bicchiere: a multimedia CD-ROM for students of Italian* to teach Italian language, history and society (Orsini-Jones, Tandy, & Rossi, 1998) which was the first example of student-informed integrated language/content hypermedia for the higher education sector in the UK.

The arrival of the World Wide Web in the late 1990s and the invention of campus-wide virtual learning environments management systems enabled me to better develop my 'vision' of student-centred CALL, trialling new approaches to teaching translation (Orsini-Jones, 2002) and language awareness (Orsini-Jones, 2004). It was thanks to these new technologies that I could co-create, in collaboration with a colleague in Health and Social Sciences, a constructivist e-learning model, the *FREE* (Fluid-Role Evolving Environment[1]). The birth of e-portfolios in the 00s enabled me to further explore how to develop language-specific study skills and critical meta-reflective competencies.

3. How has contact with colleagues impacted on the way you use technology in language learning and teaching?

The annual e-learning symposia at Southampton were fundamental for my professional development. These gatherings offered opportunities to reflect on the added value of integrating technology in language learning and teaching, to disseminate my work and to obtain valuable feedback on it from an 'expert' community of practice.

---

1. https://books.google.co.uk/books?isbn=1902454138

4. How do you use technology in your professional practice now?

There are some principles that have always underpinned my position towards technology-enhanced language learning and which have been reinforced by the dialogue had at the e-learning symposia between 2005 and 2015. Firstly, I still use technology to co-construct knowledge with my students and try and choose the best e-learning tools there are for this purpose within the constraints imposed by the ethical requirements of my institution.

Secondly, I believe that there are appropriate technological tools that can be integrated into language learning to enhance multilingual and multimodal critical digital literacies, foster meta-reflection and provide unique opportunities for social-collaboration on tasks. There are also tools that can provide innovative ways of helping students to 'Focus on Form' (e.g. Socrative.com multiple choice exercises on SMART phones).

Thirdly, I currently teach international trainee language teachers and am acutely aware of the fact that no generalisations should be made about levels of digital literacy amongst language tutors and that the e-learning up-skilling of language teachers is uneven and patchy across the globe. This presents me with a dilemma about e-learning in general and the integration/use of technology in particular. I agree with Kumaravadivelu (2012) that each language teacher will need to operate within the parameters of particularity, possibility and practicality linked to their own context (p.12). I have thus become a little reluctant to provide strong recommendations as to the best technological tools to use. While new technologies offer some exciting opportunities, they also present us with new threats, especially in regard to data protection and long-term sustainability.

Finally, both students and staff must learn to manage their social media presence and, in this globalised world, hone their *netiquette* and intercultural skills in each of the languages they communicate with. In my opinion, this is one of the main e-learning challenges for the academic and professional development of the linguists of the future.

5. How does your knowledge and experience in social media and web 2.0 technologies impact on your professional and teaching life?

5.1. Current projects in telecollaboration

I believe that language learning and teaching should reflect current research findings in the field and that both cognitive theories and interactional/sociolinguistic/sociosemantic ones should be taken into account when trying to understand how languages are learnt. Evidence has been emerging that seems to substantiate the claim that linguistic proficiency and Intercultural Communicative Competence (ICC) –pragmatic competence in the target language in particular– can be enhanced by the use of Computer Mediated Communication (CMC), as is well summarised by O'Dowd (2013) reporting on the findings of research on telecollaboration.

I am currently engaging in large-scale action-research-informed telecollaborative projects that are fully integrated into the first year curriculum and form part of the assessment of a ten credit mandatory module at Coventry University. There are many models of telecollaboration (see O'Dowd, 2013); I have been developing a 'hybrid' one, where students have opportunities to be exposed to and to practise interaction both in the target language studied and English used as a lingua franca, while reflecting on tailor-made intercultural tasks. In keeping with my focus on multilingual and multimodal multiliteracies, this model aims to develop cyberpragmatics, defined by Yus (2011) as the skill in understanding others' intended meanings in computer-mediated communication. Cyberpragmatics includes, for example, gauging the correct level of formality, developing the ability to switch between registers and genres and interpreting intended meanings.

The integration of telecollaboration into the curriculum is also enabling me to address the need to comply with governmental and institutional drives, such as the internationalisation of the curriculum to foster the competence of 'global graduatedness' in its neoliberal connotations of 'global employability'.

At the same time, I am finding that telecollaboration is making it possible to encourage both students and staff to become aware of the social justice connotation of 'global graduatedness', as the fostering of the respect for the 'different other'.

Figure 1. Framework for the goals of telecollaboration 2.0
(Helm & Guth, 2010[1], p. 74)

New Online Literacies	ICC	Foreign Language Learning
Operational: The "technical stuff"		
Computer literacy Information literacies New media literacies	*Savoir apprendre/faire:* Skills of discovery and interaction *Savoir comprendre:* ability to interpret a document or event from another culture, to explain it and relate it to one's own	Spoken production Spoken interaction Written production Reading Listening Codeswitching
Operational: Attitude: the "ethos stuff"		
Willingness to explore, learn from, participate in, and collaborate and share in online communities	*Savoir-etre:* attitude of openness and curiosity	Autonomy Motivation Willingness to communicate
Cultural		
Knowledge of literacy practises and appropriate ways of communicating online Propositional knowledge of topic	*Savoirs:* knowledge of social groups and their products and practices in own and other cultures; knowledge of the processes of interaction	Linguistic knowledge Sociolinguistic knowledge Pragmatic knowledge
Critical		
Critical Literacy Awareness	Critical Cultural Awareness	Critical Language Awareness

In my experience, telecollaborative projects can be complex, challenging and troublesome (Orsini-Jones et al., in press). But real learning involves being taken out of one's 'comfort zone'. Moreover, active and critical participation in telecollaboration facilitated by web 2.0 tools encompasses a variety of competences for a language learner –and a language teacher (see Figure 1 above

---

[1]. Reproduced with kind permission from the authors

by Helm & Guth, 2010) that make it worth engaging with. In the keynote presentation I gave at the 2014 LLAS e-learning symposium[1], I argued that the added value that telecollaboration can bring to the language learning and teaching environment is multifaceted and proposed that online interaction in telecollaboration exchanges in higher education is a digital multimodal genre for specific academic purposes.

5.2. The evolution of the 'Culture Canon' in language learning

Engaging with telecollaboration has enabled me to reflect on how the concept of 'culture' has evolved from the 80s to date, following the development of the definitions of communicative competence. I will illustrate this with the support of a good summary of the culture research canon provided by Weninger and Kiss (2013) who discuss it through the changed interpretation of the concept of 'culture' drawn from textbooks for English as a Foreign Language (EFL).

When I arrived in the UK in 1984, culture was seen "as an object, a set of facts to be learned about the target language culture, which in most cases entailed national culture" (Weninger & Kiss, 2013, p. 697), and mainly referred to *C*ulture with a capital *C* (e.g. literature, history, art). Language learning tended to adhere to the acculturation model requiring immersion in the foreign culture. In my plenary at the e-learning symposium in January 2014, I jokingly referred to how closely my personal language learning experience reflected this, as I came to live in the UK and married an English man. But it was not just a joke, I had 'bought' into the immersion model and even remember 'forcing' my students to change their British names to their improbable Italian equivalents (which was not easy with 'Craig' and 'Wayne', for example).

I then lived through the reconceptualisation that started from the mid-1990s, with communicative language teaching, when the 'Cultural artefact' was

---

[1]. See a recording at https://coursecast.soton.ac.uk/Panopto/Pages/Viewer.aspx?id=96110436-d00d-4d61-9340-9aa3b910b7b

substituted with "*c*ulture with a small *c*" (Weninger & Kiss, 2013, p. 697), e.g. popular culture. Language and culture were seen as complementary for successful language acquisition and the focus moved to "inter-, cross-, and transcultural issues in language teaching in order to develop intercultural communicative competence" (Weninger & Kiss, 2013, p. 697) (see the ICC section in Helm & Guth, 2010 above).

It can be argued that technological change (the advent of the World Wide Web) drove the major cultural shift (still) occurring from around 2000 to date that has characterised the perception of what 'intercultural competence' is nowadays. This new concept of culture in language learning and teaching is associated with postmodern tenets and the development of intercultural critical citizenship on a global scale (Kumaravadivelu, 2012).

Although this summary is based on the way the culture canon has influenced the design of EFL textbooks, I am embracing telecollaboration because I agree with Godwin-Jones (2013) that it is rather difficult for language learning textbooks to provide a rich mix of critical intercultural exposure (p. 2). They often propose a vision of culture that is superficial and has a tourist-inspired perspective.

Telecollaboration provides a unique opportunity for contact with other cultures on a global scale. It is telling in a way that telecollaboration is currently being adopted by other subjects and we linguists have led the way in this field of e-learning. Telecollaboration has become OIL (Online Intercultural Learning/ Online International Learning) and gone 'mainstream', beyond its initial language-specific theorisation.

However, I have a word of warning that my experience of telecollaboration has taught me. The evolution of the conceptualisation of culture discussed above and the consequent changes to pedagogical tenets adopted (mainly) in the WASP (White, Anglo-Saxon and Protestant) higher education language learning and teaching world have not necessarily been adopted in the countries we are telecollaborating with. This can lead to pedagogical intercultural critical incidents.

Chapter 4

5.3. Telecollaboration through the 'looking glass' of the expert students' eyes

In keeping with my previous model of 'role-reversal' CALL, a distinctive feature of the telecollaborative projects that we are carrying out at Coventry University consists of the fact that I hire expert undergraduate and postgraduate students as co-researchers. The model (see Figure 2 below) is driven by cycles of action-research and also draws from the transactional educational inquiry theory known as *threshold-concept pedagogy*[1] . The expert students are helping with identifying troublesome telecollaborative concepts and exploring ways to support their peers via the design of *netiquette* activities and digital tasks with staff. It is refreshing for us –staff– to 'deconstruct' our pedagogical actions through the expert students' eyes and feedback.

Figure 2. Role-reversal model of threshold concept pedagogy in languages and linguistics[2]

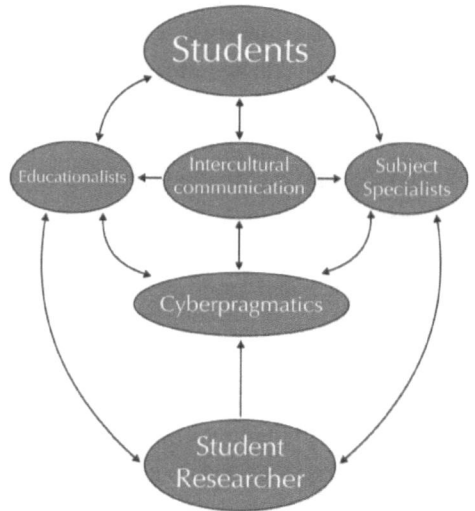

---

1. See definition at http://www.ee.ucl.ac.uk/~mflanaga/thresholds.html

2. © Orsini-Jones 2011

5.4. Telecollaborative tasks

The action-research cycles of the project taught us (the telecollaborative project team) a lesson that forced us into a 'u-turn' on task design. In the effort to abandon the role of the 'sage on stage' and empower learners, we had embraced a bottom-up approach and left students a considerable amount of choice and freedom in terms of topics to cover and tasks to carry out.

In the rather chaotic pedagogical scenario that ensued, we realised that when the development of multiliteracies at a distance is involved, a very careful scaffolding plan is needed. In the subsequent telecollaboration cycles, we structured both the activities and the online environment with the overseas partners and the expert students and also addressed our partners' dislike of Moodle's 'linearity' by designing a 'tiled' view of the learning environment: compare Figure 3 (MexCo –Mexico/Coventry– initial Moodle interface) with Figure 4 (current Moodle interface –work in progress).

Figure 3. MexCo –Mexico/Coventry– initial Moodle interface

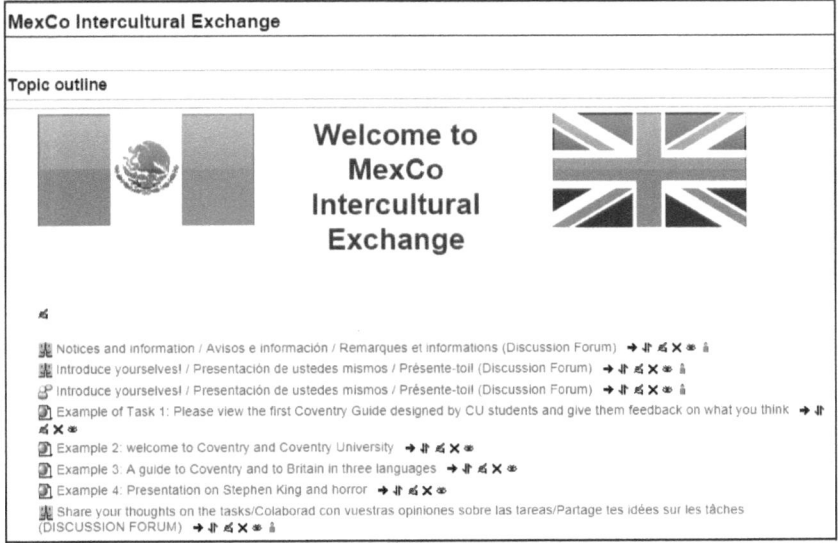

Figure 4. Current Moodle interface –work in progress

We did, however, always observe intercultural task-design guidelines drawn from relevant literature, such as Liddicoat and Scarino's (2013, pp. 57-59) who recommend the adoption of an experiential approach that includes the following 'ingredients':

- active construction;
- making connections;
- social interaction;
- reflection;
- responsibility.

The tasks we have designed are aimed at helping students to reflect on how all cultures are 'constructed' and how we can 'deconstruct' multimodal representations of culture to develop critical intercultural awareness. Students carry out the tasks using both web 1.0 (e.g. Moodle and email) and web 2.0 (e.g. Skype, Facebook, Google +, YouTube) platforms. At Coventry University, students must design a collaborative multimedia learning object based on the tasks they have engaged with using the e-portfolio Mahara[1] and present it to their tutors and peers.

---

1. https://mahara.org/

The e-tasks we designed offered participants the opportunity to develop the following multimodal and multilingual multiliteracies:

- intercultural opportunities: analysis/comparison/debate;

- linguistic opportunities: editing/translating/creating/discussing (both oral and written);

- cyberpragmatic opportunities: intercultural online discourse analysis of the forum exchanges and replies/netiquette exercises;

- multimedia learning object digital design (using the e-portfolio Mahara and YouTube);

- reflective and metareflective individual and group opportunities (commenting on one's experience/minuting progress).

5.5. Issues arising in telecollaborative projects

Between 2011 and 2014, I have been involved in telecollaboration projects with France, Germany, Israel, Mexico, Spain and Turkey. Critical incidents have occurred both amongst students and amongst staff. In my experience, web 2.0 platforms can amplify the resonance of negative critical incidents as they make them more shareable, which can in turn escalate misunderstandings.

With reference to both ourselves and our peers in other countries, what is becoming apparent is that the 'languaging' we are using for the project has different semantic connotations. Even if the words used are the same, we often discover that we do not interpret them with the same meaning, and it is not just a translation issue. The pedagogical interpretation of certain expressions and words, such as 'digital literacies', 'task', 'student-centred' and 'student autonomy' would appear to differ considerably in the UK and in Mexico, for example, at least in our experience.

Chapter 4

Another troublesome area is that of the baggage of 'tacit knowledge' (Perkins, 2006) that staff and students have. The expectations that some partners have of Britain and British students (and vice-versa) are not normally met in reality for example, and some problematic issues can ensue from this. I feel that we need more research in this sensitive area of 'pedagogical intercultural issues' in telecollaboration exchanges to better support tutors in their journey to become global citizens and 'global pedagogues'.

5.6. Summing up

In the light of the findings in the telecollaboration projects I have been involved with, I have learnt, in collaboration with my colleagues and students involved in the MexCo project, to whom I am indebted for many of the reflections reported here, that in telecollaboration it is desirable to:

- carefully scaffold the introduction to online interaction and provide many lines of digital support;

- discuss the multimodal multiliteracy demands of telecollaboration before, during and after the project with all participants involved;

- raise awareness of 'intercultural cyberpragmatic competence 2.0' (linking the blocks in Helm and Guth's (2010) model in Figure 1);

- have a dialogue with expert students to design cyberpragmatic guidelines on 'rules of telecollaborative discourse engagement' and tailor-made 'netiquette' exercises;

- test the e-learning platforms with partners before the beginning of the project;

- not make any assumptions about the level of digital literacy of the students or staff involved;

- avoid 'essentialising' and 'generalising', and provide some socio-cultural, geographical and historical information on the partners' context.

I have finally learnt that intercultural cyberpragmatic competence plays a prominent role in telecollaboration and that it must be taught to students and staff in higher education as it forms an integral part of the multilingual multimodal multiliteracies needed for global citizenship.

References

Godwin-Jones, R. (2013). Integrating intercultural competence into language learning through technology. *Language Learning & Technology, 17*(2), 1-11.

Helm, F., & Guth, S. (2010). The multifarious goals of telecollaboration 2.0: Theoretical and practical implications. In S. Guth & F. Helm (Eds), *Telecollaboration 2.0* (pp. 69-106). Bern: Peter Lang.

Kumaravadivelu, B. (2012). *Language teacher education for a global society*. Abingdon: Routledge.

Liddicoat, A. J., & Scarino, A. (2013). *Intercultural language teaching and learning*. Chichester: Wiley Blackwell. doi:10.1002/9781118482070

Orsini-Jones, M., Tandy, V., & Rossi, N. (Eds). (1998). *La neve nel bicchiere: A multimedia CD-ROM for students of Italian*. Coventry: Coventry University/Camsoft.

Orsini-Jones, M. (2002). Teaching translation with the help of computers: The added value of hypertextuality. In G. Talbot & P. Williams (Eds), *Essays in learning, language, translation and the digital learning technologies* (pp. 57-67). Leicestershire: Troubador Publishing Ltd.

Orsini-Jones, M. (2004). Supporting a course in new literacies and skills for linguists with a virtual learning environment: Results from a staff/student collaborative action-research project at Coventry University. *ReCALL, 16*(1), 189-209. doi: 10.1017/S0958344004001417

Orsini-Jones, M., Lloyd, E., Gazeley, Z., Lopez-Vera, B., Pibworth, L., & Bescond, G. (in press). Student-driven intercultural awareness raising with MexCo: Agency, autonomy and threshold concepts in a telecollaborative project between the UK and Mexico. In R. O'Dowd, M. Dooley, & N. Tcherepashenets (Eds), *Telecollaboration and lessons in world citizenship*. Bern/NY: Peter Lang.

O'Dowd, R. (2013). Telecollaboration and CALL. In M. Thomas, H. Reinders, & M. Warschauer (Eds), *Contemporary computer-assisted language learning* (pp. 123-139). London/New York: Bloomsbury.

Perkins, D. (2006). Constructivism and troublesome knowledge. In J. H. E. Meyer & R. Land (Eds), *Overcoming barriers to student understanding: Threshold concepts and troublesome knowledge* (pp. 33-47). London: RoutledgeFalmer.

Weninger, C., & Kiss, T. (2013). Culture in English as a foreign language (EFL) textbooks: A semiotic approach. *TESOL quarterly, 47*(4), 694-716. doi:10.1002/tesq.87

Yus, F. (2011). *Cyberpragmatics: Internet-mediated communication in context.* Amsterdam / Philadelphia: John Benjamins

5. Learning to swim in new waters: A meta-narrative about the design and implementation of a virtual learning environment for language learning and teaching

Teresa MacKinnon[1]

Abstract

In the past 5 years, the Language Centre at the University of Warwick has designed and implemented a blended learning environment in order to meet two important challenges to our Institution-Wide Language Programme (IWLP) language teaching mission. These were to connect teachers and learners together online in order to better support progress where class contact time was limited, and to provide effective support to teaching colleagues with little or no experience of e-learning. Designing the portal, known as Languages@Warwick, involved a complex process of needs analysis, technical and financial understanding and interaction with many stakeholders. Progress in the use of the platform was regularly reviewed and shared with the tutor community in order to inform next steps. This chapter will present an emerging understanding of the nature and impact of the developments set against the rapidly changing technological and pedagogical landscape. One which can perhaps best be described not as a community of practice, as had been expected, but rather as a collection of participatory communities known as collectives.

Keywords: community of practice, collective, CPD, telecollaboration, e-portfolio, VLE, open practice.

---

1. University of Warwick, United Kingdom; t.mackinnon@warwick.ac.uk.

How to cite this chapter: MacKinnon, T. (2015). Learning to swim in new waters: A meta-narrative about the design and implementation of a virtual learning environment for language learning and teaching. In K. Borthwick, E. Corradini, & A. Dickens (Eds), *10 years of the LLAS elearning symposium: Case studies in good practice* (pp. 57-66). Dublin: Research-publishing.net. doi:10.14705/rpnet.2015.000267

Chapter 5

1. Context/rationale

> "In the new culture of learning, people learn through their interaction and participation with one another in fluid relationships that are the result of shared interests and opportunity" (Thomas & Seeley Brown, 2011, p. 50).

For Millennials[1], those who have grown up with access to digital communication technologies and who thrive in a culture greatly mediated through the internet, it is unthinkable that their learning would not include use of internet affordances and easy access to important resources wherever they are. It is unsurprising therefore that from 2000 onwards the Warwick Language Centre was increasingly receiving student feedback expressing a need for greater online support beyond the classroom. Few tutors in those early days were meeting those expressed needs, and those who were found trying to exploit the institutional provision (an in-house web text editor) both frustrating and time consuming. The system did not support international character and script use and was very manual in nature requiring considerable time in setup and management. Many tutors were hourly paid or part time and simply did not feel the need to invest additional time in such efforts given that they could show websites in class and email links to their students.

With a new director recently arrived, a decision was taken to investigate the implementation of a Virtual Learning Environment (VLE) for the centre's teaching. This had to be achieved with limited financial and human resources given that such a system was not provided by the institution. The project lead was an early adopter of technologies for learning and, after consulting with the head of IT services, undertook a local needs analysis. Wider information gathering involved the e-learning community through literature reviews, JISCMail and conversations with peers in the sector's language teaching community, such as the Association for University Language Centres, in order to assist the decision making process.

---

1. Millenials: http://en.wikipedia.org/wiki/Millennials

2. Aims and objectives

An e-learning strategy was put in place, prioritising:

- the provision of suitable, easy to use tools to facilitate language development;

- opportunities for professional development for our language tutors.

It was clear there was a need to provide for blended learning and, as this was a new departure for Centre staff, to support tutor development, both technical and methodological, in a way that did not penalise those already engaged in innovative pedagogical design.

A hosted implementation of Moodle was set up in the summer of 2011 as a pilot for 300 students and a small, enthusiastic number of staff participants. Within the pilot implementation of Languages@Warwick all participating staff were given access to language specific sandbox courses with teacher rights and a course known as *101: Using Moodle for Language Teaching*, moderated by the lead practitioner. Here participants could experience the site as a student, accessing tutor guides and 'how to' resources, connecting to each other through a forum to report any issues or concerns. This phase was vital to informing the next stages of development through the collection of qualitative and quantitative data. The experiences of all involved resulted in greater insights into the activities most tutors felt were significant and the aspects of Moodle that were the most challenging for tutors with little technical experience.

3. What I did

Subsequent annual iterations of Languages@Warwick continued with this same action research approach. The platform was extended to cover all Language Centre programmes and some external collaborations. There was a user base of around 4,000 people. We were then able to formalise the technical support structure by appointing a Technology Integrator (initially part-time). We replaced most of our geographically situated technical provision (such as fixed language labs) with online interaction through Languages@Warwick. The project lead and a small group of tutors had been investigating the use of voice over the internet using Wimba[1] tools and presented their findings on tailored listening provision through an online presentation for Edulearn in 2011[2]. The technologies used for audio and video files are generally large files which can be difficult to manage as they affect the functioning of the Moodle course. The complexity of file types and their dependence upon certain codecs and software being available for playback can be confusing for users. Designing opportunities for interaction can also be time consuming and may not get anticipated engagement. Such factors were part of the learning process which informed the tool choices in Languages@ Warwick. The lead found technical help and inspiration through the Association for Learning Technology and completed a professional certification to qualify as a Certified Member of the Association for Learning technologies (CMALT) holder, a professional accreditation scheme for learning technologists.

Other tutors who had been keen to develop their use of technology continued to enhance their course environments using the tools provided in Languages@ Warwick, which by 2012 included an e-portfolio tool (Mahara), collaboration and communication tools (Blackboard Collaborate classrooms, Instant Messenger and voice tools), and from 2013 a streaming media solution (Kaltura). A course review revealed high levels of tutor video use for language learning which merited technical management as described in a Jisc Digital Media case study[3].

A further group of our international tutors were willing to experiment with e-portfolio assessment and the resultant project, which drew on work by Jisc, developed a set of assessment criteria published openly in Scribd which had been created and modified collaboratively. This e-portfolio project is now in its fourth year and involves over 100 students in 5 different languages: Chinese, Japanese, German, French and Spanish. Regular participation in dissemination

---

1. Technology provider later acquired by Blackboard, now known as Blackboard Collaborate.

2. Edulearn 2011 https://www.youtube.com/watch?v=iRi0dnSWfKI&feature=youtu.be&list=UUzIsBh-a_JyXNqECzw7PF2g

3. JISC case study http://www.jiscdigitalmedia.ac.uk/casestudy/language-centre-university-of-warwick

opportunities presented by LLAS[1] conferences and e-learning symposia facilitated the consolidation of our e-learning networks due to the open nature of the dissemination.

During this development phase, the significance of social networks and informal learning became apparent to the project lead, who began to actively connect with other educators and 'edtech' specialists using Twitter and YouTube channels. Social networking tools provide an efficient way of disseminating teacher tutorials and became a personal learning environment for the lead's professional development as reported in the LLAS journal, Liaison (MacKinnon, 2012). The impact of social networking tools should not be underestimated and was instrumental in further growth, bringing elements of coincidence and serendipity. A virtual exchange (Clavier) emerged from a chance online conversation with an educator based in France and this in turn led to greater involvement in investigation of tools for telecollaboration and asynchronous interaction. The Clavier virtual exchange was included as a case study in the EU funded Intent report[2]. Warwick's virtual exchange is now in its 4th year. Over 900 students were involved last year and the project continues to impact on both physical mobility and curriculum design. This engagement in technology for telecollaboration also led to new opportunities as the project lead was invited by the Higher Education Academy to prepare a report on e-tools for international collaborations[3].

A recent analysis of the role of the online spaces shared by Clavier (the EWC course) available through Languages@Warwick used a tool developed by Mark Childs (2008), the MERM framework, surfacing the aspects of the space that contribute to lowering barriers to engagement and participation. The MERM framework is a conceptual framework which merges the two models available in *activity theory* and *community of practice*, providing a basis for the systematic review of the various aspects of activity through

---

1. Language Futures, July 2012; 8th Annual e-learning symposium, January 2013; Reshaping Languages in Higher Education, July 2014, University of Southampton.

2. http://www.intent-project.eu/?q=node/34

3. http://www.ucml.ac.uk/sites/default/files/pages/160/Using_e_tools.pdf

Chapter 5

mediated environments (Childs, 2008). Using the descriptors from MERM, it was possible to identify aspects of the environment that could be controlled as part of the design of the environment and those which were dependent upon the attributes of the individual user and therefore would benefit from more personal support from tutors and mentors (see Table 1).

Table 1.   MERM applied to Languages@Warwick EWC course

contributing factors to experience of mediated environment		relevance to Clavier and EWC activity
characteristics of participant	degree of naturalisation	especially difficult for Clermont (France), students, but also unfamiliarity with VLE use at Warwick
	tendency (narrative, immersive etc.)	individual difference
roles and conventions	maximising co-presence	synchronous tools and activities available to reduce this, used mainly by staff
	relationship to environment	access locations differed, French students had access during class time, English students had limited class time and were expected to engage during their own time
	relationship to technology	technology choices appropriate, no significant technological restraints and support was available (e.g. video clip tutorials)
learning activity	teaching approach	greater diversity as team increases, tasks well designed
	teaching technique	greater diversity as team increases, staff familiarity with the purpose of the exchange has evolved over time
	stage in presence development	this was considered in task sequence design, graduating tasks in complexity over time
community	trajectory	launch event at Warwick to raise awareness, institutional publicity in Clermont
	boundaries	open and fluid, this was a fundamental premise
presence (situated experience)	mediated presence (the sense of being somewhere else)	open - synchronous and asynchronous, language use (French/English) not stipulated, students free to communicate however they felt appropriate and to use media such as images and video
	social presence (ability to project oneself)	lots of opportunities for informal connections e.g. Twitter, FB, FIFA tournament, initial activity centres on creation of a profile
	co-presence (sense of being together)	availability of Instant Messenger and online classroom to increase this, sharing of external activity back into EWC builds visibility of interaction

characteristics of environment	embodiment	profile creation activity, students not restricted in choice of avatar, supported to reflect on appropriate representation
	realness	institutional platform but with holes in the walls, acceptance that students may prefer their own tools
	interactivity	tasks designed to promote both formal and informal learning
	unobtrusiveness	French students had to email in English to get technical support
	persistence	increased by using communication channels such as Facebook and Twitter
	communication channels	most effective when communication moves into students' own channels
	navigation	most challenging for French students but also Warwick students had to access Mahara through Languages@Warwick and cope with a new navigation
	narrative	aggregation tools (storify, RSS feeds) used to emphasise this in EWC
identity	concept of self	students were encouraged to discuss as part of setting up profile
	representation of self	most engaged to some extent and had well developed profiles across networks, reports of continued interaction beyond the end of the course
	aspects of self	individual difference

As stated earlier, the project lead embarked upon this learning process with an open mind set. Using social media and curation tools allowed us to share learning online under a Creative Commons licence. This approach has helped in ensuring that peer feedback and support beyond the institution has been incorporated in the design process. Artefacts created during the ongoing developments are shared through a YouTube channel[1], Kaltura galleries[2], a G+ community, slideshare[3] and other social networking tools. From the outset, it was important that our VLE Languages@Warwick should be a walled garden with holes! The notion of rhizomatic[4] learning became central to our international collaborations and has engendered an emerging international

---

1. Warwick Language YouTube channel: https://www.youtube.com/channel/UCzIsBh-a_JyXNqECzw7PF2g
2. Warwick Kaltura Galleries: https://warwick.mediaspace.kaltura.com/category/Resources/6610831
3. Slideshare: http://www.slideshare.net/teresamac
4. http://www.open.edu/openlearn/education/open-education/content-section-7.5

network of teacher educators, re-purposing the #Clavier name. The nascent network was presented at Eurocall in August 2014. There is still much to realise in order to achieve the vision of openness in education, there are many interests which may resist realisation of openness, but this grass roots example of open practice is a good illustration of Weller's (2011) "Little OER" (p. 109) and the benefits that it can bring.

4. Discussion

The development of Languages@Warwick has brought with it many unexpected consequences. Local administration of the VLE has facilitated greater flexibility in shared access to courses, allowing wider collaborations beyond our institution which, in turn, have brought helpful connections for our professional development. One should not underestimate the value of such localisation at a time when teachers often feel relegated to mere content providers for an institutional 'e-learning solution'. Languages@Warwick design allows for a wide range of learning scenarios from the minimal to the innovative and this means the tutor or 'lead learner' can experiment with the technologies and implement the best ones for their learning design as and when they are comfortable. Effective practice is recognised and shared in regular institutional and departmental gatherings. The community of practice approach to our development was evaluated recently in a paper delivered at Eurocall Evora in 2013 (MacKinnon, 2013). This highlighted the nature of learning that can be facilitated in flexible spaces such as our 'holey' walled garden, particularly when the affordances of social networks are also exploited offering informal learning. A marriage between structure and freedom, as described by Thomas and Seeley Brown (2011), helps us to embrace change in a rapidly changing context, moving from a teaching-based approach to a learning-based approach. All participants are able to contribute to extending the learning environment beyond the classroom and traditional roles of teacher and learner become irrelevant as all explore together. Further research carried out into the engagement of students through the Clavier course EWC (to be published) also points to behaviour which is better described as that of a collective rather than a community:

"Communities derive their strength from creating a sense of belonging, while collectives derive theirs from participation" (Thomas & Seely Brown, 2011, p. 52).

5. Conclusion

The new waters teaching professionals are navigating are bringing changes and demands we are yet to fully understand. The ever expanding modes of communication and varieties of technologies for learning challenge us to explore them in order to better understand their affordances. We can only hope to swim in these currents if we are prepared to get our feet wet! The past 4 years have seen an increasing adoption of technology for learning by all our tutors and we have been able to analyse the data around these developments in order to inform our next steps. During the summer of 2014 we have migrated our Languages@ Warwick site to a new, more robust implementation of Moodle, Moodlerooms Joule. This has brought many advantages, specifically:

- greater access to data for all users, not just site administrators;

- more sophisticated learning tools such as the Personalised Learning designer to tailor course design to individual users;

- an integrated badging system for Open Badges;

- comprehensive user support through a knowledge base of tutorials and how-to documents.

The new site will continue to be subjected to our user feedback and evaluations as we maintain this constant learning process. Lifelong learning is fundamental to professional development and we continue to prioritise the importance of community engagement, learning from each other in interest driven collectives. The coming year will see broader emphasis upon open educational practice and the value of sharing, working towards mainstreaming this aspect of tutor practice through the implementation of a central repository (Equella), which helps to make contributed VLE content searchable and available under CC-BY licence both within and beyond our context. Downes' (2009) 'get out of the way' position advocates a focus on removing boundaries to collaboration, and the approach we are adopting draws upon Weller's (2011) "A Pedagogy of Abundance" (p. 85) (see Hoyle, 2009 for an account of Weller's idea). Languages@Warwick has enabled our voyages to new horizons[1] and the dissemination of that learning is an important contribution to meeting the challenges facing the international language teaching community.

References

Childs, M. (2008). Using a mediated environments reference model to evaluate learners' experiences of Second Life. In *Proceedings of the 6th International Conference on Networked Learning, 5-6 May 2008, Greece*. Retrieved from http://www.networkedlearningconference.org.uk/past/nlc2008/abstracts/Childs.htm

Downes, S. (2009). *Downes-Wiley: A conversation on open educational resources*. Retrieved from http://www.downes.ca/files/books/Downes-Wiley.pdf

Hoyle, M. A. (2009). *OER and a pedagogy of abundance*. Retrieved from http://einiverse.eingang.org/2009/11/18/oer-and-a-pedagogy-of-abundance/

MacKinnon, T. (2012). Social media for Language Teachers. In E. Hudswell (Ed.), Liaison Magazine, Issue 7: June 2012 (pp. 20-21). Southampton: LLAS Centre. Retrieved from https://www.llas.ac.uk/sites/default/files/nodes/179/LLAS_Liaison_Magazine_Issue_7_SMALL.pdf

MacKinnon, T. (2013). Creating and nurturing a community of practice for language teachers in Higher Education. In L. Bradley & S. Thouësny (Eds), *20 Years of EUROCALL: Learning from the Past, Looking to the Future* (pp. 175-182). Dublin Ireland: Research-publishing.net. doi:10.14705/rpnet.2013.000157

Thomas, D., & Seely Brown, J. (2011). *A new culture of learning: Cultivating the imagination for a world of constant change*. CreateSpace Independent Publishing Platform.

Weller, M. (2011). *The Digital Scholar*. London: Bloomsbury.

---

1. ALT-C 2014 presentation: voyages to new horizons http://altc.alt.ac.uk/conference/2014/sessions/voyages-to-new-horizons-526/

6. From autonomous to peer e-learning – How the FReE Team turned ePortfolio into a social network between first and final-year modern languages students

Jean-Christophe Penet[1]

Abstract

In this case study, I will show how I redesigned the curriculum of a post-A Level French module in order to improve students' career awareness and their soft –interpersonal and transferable– skills through autonomous e-learning. In the first phase of the project (2012/13), students were encouraged to start thinking in French about their career ambitions by making use of the University's ePortfolio. The feedback from this phase showed that the dual objective to boost students' linguistic progress while making them more career aware had been reached, but that their motivation, however, tended to flag over time, especially in semester 2. A second phase of the project (2013/14) therefore aimed to remedy this by turning ePortfolio into a social networking site between first- and final-year students. Blending peer-learning with e-learning, the team of final-years was tasked with giving the project a real presence on ePortfolio by replying to the first-year's posts on employability. It is believed that FRE1071 students' motivation was increased by the team of final-year students' open dialogue with first-years about their employability tasks on ePortfolio.

Keywords: e-learning , employability, autonomy, motivation, peer learning, mentoring.

---

1. University of Newcastle, United Kingdom; jean-christophe.penet@newcastle.ac.uk.

How to cite this chapter: Penet, J.-C. (2015). From autonomous to peer e-learning – How the FReE Team turned ePortfolio into a social network between first and final-year modern languages students. In K. Borthwick, E. Corradini, & A. Dickens (Eds), *10 years of the LLAS elearning symposium: Case studies in good practice* (pp. 67-75). Dublin: Research-publishing.net. doi:10.14705/rpnet.2015.000268

Chapter 6

1. Context/rationale

This case study takes place in the context of FRE1071, a first-year post-A Level French module (level B1-B2 ECFRL[1]) offered by Newcastle University's School of Modern Languages (SML). This module presents two main pedagogical challenges. First of all, it consists of students from different academic backgrounds as it welcomes both SML students reading French and students from other Schools –mostly Business and Politics– who would like to pursue their studies of the language. What is more, FRE1071 is a large module with some 100 students joining it every year. To cater for such an audience, FRE1071 comprises of a weekly lecture followed by a two-hour seminar where listening and speaking skills are practised in small groups. As a result of this, weekly homework is the main way for students to improve their French written skills. This implies that students learn to negotiate the transition from small A-Level language groups in which they received a lot of individualised feedback to a more autonomous way of learning French in a less controlled environment.

For many students, such a shift can prove challenging. However, to language instructors, it can represent an opportunity to increase their students' motivation for language learning. Indeed, second language (L2) acquisition researcher Ema Ushioda (2011) makes the point that, until recently, "L2 motivation research has been more concerned with idealised language learners as theoretical abstractions [...] rather than with learners as uniquely complex individual 'people' with particular social identities, situated in particular contexts" (p. 222). This goes against education psychology that has shown that "motivation is not necessarily achievement oriented but value-based and identity-oriented" (Ushioda, 2011, p. 221). Hence the need to "move away from achievement-oriented analyses of motivation to *identity-oriented analyses of personal motivational trajectories*" (Ushioda, 2011, p. 222). Hence, too, the pivotal role played by autonomy in language learning as it constitutes "a way of encouraging students to experience that sense of personal agency and

---

1. European Common Framework of Reference for Languages

self-determination that is vital to developing their motivation from within" (Ushioda, 2011, p. 224).

It is easy to see the appeal of Ushioda's (2011) theory in the context of FRE1071, as it encourages autonomy not as a result of limited resources but as a way of better catering for students from varied backgrounds by increasing their motivation for language learning. In the first phase of the project (2012/13), I therefore decided to review the syllabus so as to give students a greater sense of agency through the completion of autonomous, value-based and identity-oriented tasks in French. To do so, I designed autonomous tasks focusing on students' –projected– professional identity in collaboration with the University's Careers Service. These tasks, which linked with some of the module activities and school-wide career events, represented an opportunity for students to start thinking in French about potential future career paths and reflect on how the skills they were developing through their language studies could help them achieve their objectives. This followed recommendation eight of the Worton Review on languages, according to which "Modern Foreign Language Departments should work more proactively on skills development and careers advice and guidance" (HEFCE, 2009, p. 37). To try and make them engaging, I decided to ask students to complete the employability tasks on what was then a new platform launched by the University to help students increase their employability, ePortfolio. ePortfolio was first set up with the objective of encouraging students to log and exemplify all the graduate skills they develop during the course of their studies at Newcastle University and it therefore appeared to be the perfect platform for the project.

The impact of this first phase of the project on students was assessed by two end-of-semester questionnaires, Q1 and Q2. They achieved response rates of 78% and 70% respectively. In Q1 and Q2, 89% and 84% of students respectively found the opportunity to reflect critically on how some course activities may have contributed to their professional development 'useful' or 'very useful.' The slight drop between Q1 and Q2 could be explained by the fact that the employability tasks students had to complete on ePortfolio in semester two no longer related directly to in-class activities. This was in the hope that it would encourage students to work more autonomously. What is more, 96% (Q1) and 90% (Q2) of students said that the tasks were 'useful' or 'very useful' in terms of language development. Here again, however, we can see a slight drop between both semesters which may be explained by the greater autonomy given to students concerning the tasks in semester two. Even though 78% of respondents agreed that the project was a 'positive development' for FRE1071 (Q1 and Q2), the questionnaires showed that students found it easier to grasp the linguistic benefit of the tasks than their benefit in terms of career awareness and that motivation tended to drop in the second semester.

I shared these results at the 8th Annual LLAS eLearning Symposium in January 2013 and the discussion that ensued with colleagues confirmed the need to turn ePortfolio into a social network by integrating an element of peer learning to e-learning in the second phase of the project.

2. Aims and objectives

Funded by Newcastle University's Innovation Fund and launched in June 2013, this new phase aimed to increase first-year students' motivation by setting up a team of three final-year students in charge of giving first-year students individualised feedback on their ePortfolio tasks that would address both language and content. The aims and objectives were to:

- enhance FRE1071 students' motivation by improving the feedback received on their ePortfolio tasks both quantitatively and qualitatively;

- develop FRE1071 students' awareness of the importance of engaging with career-related issues early on in their studies through online interaction with final-year students;

- enhance the motivation of final-year students by giving them some agency in the SML and enhance their employability through their role in the project.

3. What I did

I first recruited three final-year students and asked them to review all of the tasks, the use of ePortfolio and create a sense of community for the project. Choosing final-years to act as mentors on the project looked like the best option despite their heavy workload. First of all, they were all already familiar with ePortfolio as they had to use it to communicate with their personal tutors in the School during their third year abroad. What is more, they had all spent their year abroad working either as British Council teaching assistants or on work placements. They had thus gained invaluable work experience, which made them more conscious of employability issues.

The Team Leader was employed through the University's work experience scheme and was tasked with setting up and organising the team. Once in place, the team unanimously decided to keep ePortfolio as the platform for the tasks as they recognised that its functionalities allowed for a real exchange among peers. By then, ePortfolio was no longer just a repository of graduates' skill development but, much more, an online tool through which students are encouraged to reinforce their reflective practice through personal blogs which they can share with others and by setting up specific communities to share and support group work and discussion with other students and staff (NUVision, 2014). Once it was confirmed that ePortfolio remained the best platform for the project, the team came up with a new name for the tasks and the team, namely "FReE" (French ePortfolio Employability) Tasks and "FReE Team" respectively. They designed a logo to help give the project more visibility and a stronger sense of community and they spent the summer working on a "FReE Tasks User Guide" and an "ePortfolio Technical Guide" so that first-year students would know exactly what was expected of them and would not encounter too many technical problems. They also reviewed the tasks in light of the 2012/13 cohort's feedback so as to tailor them better to students' needs and came up with a new set of tasks that signposted to students the skills they were practicing such as, for example, FReE Tasks 2 and 4[1] (Table 1).

---

1. Originally in French; my own translation.

Table 1. FReE Tasks 2 and 4

Skills you are practicing: • Presentation skills • Analytical skills • Group discussion **What we are looking for:** • Precise examples • Grammar, language and structure • Improvements on the points the FReE Team gave in their feedback	**FReE Task 2: 150-200 words in French** Reviewing the Dragon Den-style presentation you gave in last week's seminar (or the ones you saw if you were a Dragon) and integrating the advice given in the video on Blackboard ('How to give a good pitch'), please say what makes, according to you, a good professional presentation and how you could/would improve on your performance in future presentations.
Skills you are practising: • Extended writing in French • Analytical skills • Increased awareness of professional strengths and areas for improvement **What we are looking for:** • Improvement of points raised by FReE Team • Focussed responses to points • Improvement in grammar, language and structure.	**FReE Task 4: Value Exercise - 200 words minimum in French** The objective of this FReE Task is for you to get to know your professional selves better. Answer the following questions in French and in a minimum of 200 words: • Professionally, what kind of person am I? What are my strengths and weaknesses? • What do I excel at (e.g. sorting or thinking on my feet in difficult circumstances etc.)? • What am I interested in and what bores me the most? • Which career path(s) am I particularly keen on?

Finally, as feedback is a sensitive issue, the whole team received training and guidance on best practice in the field with the help of the University's Centre for Quality in Learning and Teaching. Concerning language accuracy, FReE Team members were asked not to correct every single mistake but to point out error patterns that individual students should address. They were also asked to encourage their peers to become more career aware in the process. The feedback was posted on ePortfolio as a reply to first-years' blog entries, as in the following example originally posted in French (FReE Task 4):

"Hi X. It looks like you are well aware of your own strengths and weaknesses. You have very useful skills for the job market –mostly your ability to work both independently and in a team. If you'd like a career in journalism, why not get some experience already by writing for the

University's paper *The Courier*? For your next blog, please try to mind accents and not to use too many commas, especially in front of 'et'. Concerning your difficulties with French vocabulary, I'd say that reading lots in French is the way to go –that's perfect for you considering that you love French literature! [...]. X"[1].

4. Discussion

As you can see from the above post, the informal tone used by final-year students to give feedback on students' blogs on ePortfolio paved the way for a real dialogue among students. The objective was, indeed, to boost first-year students' motivation for the tasks while encouraging autonomy.

The evaluation questionnaire for this phase of the project (Q3), which was returned by 64% of FRE1071 students, can give us a better idea as to whether this objective was achieved or not. First of all, 73% of respondents said that ePortfolio worked well as a place on which to upload their tasks. This was a huge increase on Q2, where only 42% of respondents thought so. This may be due to the fact that the FReE Team gave first-year students more guidance on how to use ePortfolio and turned it into a social network. This seems confirmed by the fact that 77% of respondents said it was 'useful' or 'very useful' to get feedback from their peers (Q3). 69% of them also claimed that they had tried to improve based on this feedback (Q3).From these results, one could argue that the FReE Team successfully motivated students to try and improve the quality of their autonomous work on ePortfolio. Surprisingly enough, however, only 57% of students saw the tasks as linguistically 'useful' or 'very useful' in Q3 as opposed to 90% in Q2. Similarly, only 31% of respondents agreed 'completely' or 'mostly' with the idea that the FReE Tasks encouraged their independent learning when 52% of them agreed 'somewhat' with the statement (Q3). It is difficult to explain such results. Could it be that the FReE Team's feedback made first-year students more aware of the improvements

---

1. Posted on ePortfolio on 16th December 2013 as a reply to a first-year's student blog entry answering FReE Task 4; my own translation.

Chapter 6

they still needed to make and discouraged some of them in the process? Did students feel that the interaction with the FReE Team no longer made it truly independent work? This perception would be perfectly legitimate as with the introduction of the FReE Team the tasks still encouraged students to work autonomously but not as independently as in the earlier phases of the project. Whatever the reasons, it should be noted that students' overall appreciation of the project in Q3 did not drop significantly. Indeed, 70% of respondents still rated the project as 'positive' in Q3. This is substantiated by positive qualitative feedback students gave on the project ("Positive as I am able to improve the quality of my written language whilst simultaneously learning about career-related issues" (Q3)) and to the FReE Team members ("Thank you very much for my feedback regarding my FReE Task. It has certainly improved my confidence"[1]).

The benefits of the project, however, were not just for first-year students but also for the three finalists who made up the FReE Team. When asked to comment on the project in a separate questionnaire (Q4), all commented positively on the impact the project had on their own linguistic development: "I have certainly improved throughout the tasks (as looking back I have noticed a few errors in my earlier posts). It has also encouraged me to revise certain things […] in order that I gave the students the correct advice" (Q4). All of them also commented on the project's impact on their employability, such as the Team Leader: "The career experience has been invaluable in securing my place with Teach First as it meant I could talk about all manner of things in the application and interview –employing a team, structuring feedback, supporting learning. It has definitely helped tenfold" (Q4).

5. Conclusion

Quite a few first-year students felt that the project was not beneficial for their linguistic development and their career awareness. Similarly, very few of them

---

[1]. Posted on ePortfolio on 18th February 2014 as a reply to a final-year student feedback on FReE Task 6.

took full advantage of the opportunity opened up by ePortfolio to interact fully with the FReE Team by, say, answering to the feedback provided and starting a real conversation. This does not mean, however, that progress was not made towards achieving the first two objectives of the project. Indeed, qualitative feedback collected in Q3 hints to the fact that some first-year students felt very motivated by the interaction with their peers. The fact, too, that so many of the respondents in Q3 claimed to have engaged with the feedback given by final-year students has to be seen as a positive sign, too.

More importantly, the project appears to be successful if we consider all students involved in it. Final-year students have clearly grown through their role: "I felt as though I was becoming a type of mentor as I was encouraging the students to join new clubs or apply for jobs and trying to make them more confident with their French. This was a part of the project that I really enjoyed as I found it rewarding to try and bolster their spirits if they were down" (Q4). Blending peer-learning to e-learning allowed for new bridges to be built between first- and final-year students that were conducive to greater motivation among all students. When this generation of first year students reach their final year in three years' time and take on the role of mentors in the project, these bridges will grow stronger and give the whole project even greater coherence. This, in turn, should boost first year students' motivation and secure their engagement with the project.

References

HEFCE. (2009). *Review of Modern Foreign Languages provision in higher education in England* (Chairman: Professor Michael Worton). London: Higher Education Funding Council for England. Retrieved from http://www.hefce.ac.uk/media/hefce1/pubs/hefce/2009/0941/09_41.pdf

NUVision. (2014). *ePortfolio*. Newcastle University. Retrieved from https://nuvision.ncl.ac.uk/Play/2791

Ushioda, E. (2011). Why autonomy? Insights from motivation theory and research. *Innovation in Language Learning and Teaching, 5*(2), 221-232. doi:10.1080/17501229.2011.577536

OER (re)use and language teachers' tacit professional knowledge: Three vignettes

Tita Beaven[1]

Abstract

The pedagogic practical knowledge that teachers use in their lessons is very difficult to make visible and often remains tacit. This chapter draws on data from a recent study and closely analyses a number of Open Educational Resources used by three language teachers at the UK Open University in order to try to capture how their use of the resources is informed by their cognitive, affective and systemic tacit professional knowledge. The chapter concludes that Open Educational Resources and practices can enable us to transform tacit knowledge into shared, commonly usable knowledge, which might result in better learning experiences and practices.

Keywords: OER, OEP, tacit professional knowledge, cognitive, affective, systemic.

1. Context/rationale

Open Educational Resources (OER) are educational resources that have an open licence or that are in the public domain. This means that anyone can copy, use, adapt and share them legally and freely. OER can be entire textbooks, assessment materials, lecture notes and other classroom resources, and are usually in a digital form (e.g. text, video, audio, etc.).

---

1. The Open University, United Kingdom; tita.beaven@open.ac.uk.

How to cite this chapter: Beaven, T. (2015). OER (re)use and language teachers' tacit professional knowledge: Three vignettes. In K. Borthwick, E. Corradini, & A. Dickens (Eds), *10 years of the LLAS elearning symposium: Case studies in good practice* (pp. 77-88). Dublin: Research-publishing.net. doi:10.14705/rpnet.2015.000269

Chapter 7

The reason OER are important is that at the heart of the OER movement is "the simple and powerful idea that the world's knowledge is a public good, and that technology in general and the World Wide Web in particular provide an extraordinary opportunity for everyone to share, use and reuse it" (Smith & Casserly, 2006, p. 10).

Petrides, Jimes, Middleton-Detzner, and Howell (2010) considered that OER "have the potential to enhance teaching and learning practices by facilitating communities of teachers who collaborate, share, discuss, critique, use, reuse and continuously improve educational content and practice" (p. 380), and this close engagement with OER is what defines Open Educational Practices (OEP). In their seminal edited book, *Opening Up Education*, Iiyoshi and Kumar (2008) argued that OER collections can enable teachers to reach a deeper understanding of how others create and reuse resources and thus "build upon one another's experience and practical knowledge" (p. 3). However, they pointed out that most pedagogic practical knowledge "is notoriously hard to make visible and portable", as it usually "remains tacit and invisible" (Iiyoshi & Kumar, 2008, p. 436). On the other hand, they argued that OEP are precisely about building the "intellectual and technical capacity for transforming 'tacit knowledge' into 'commonly usable knowledge'" (Iiyoshi & Kumar, 2008, p. 435).

My interest in this area stems from work that has been taking place in the Department of Languages at the Open University (OU) to engage with OER and to promote OEP. The OU teaches languages through a blended model of supported distance learning: students study independently but are supported by teachers. Teachers mark students' assignments and give them feedback, and also run regular classes, called tutorials. These can be face-to-face but are mostly online, through an audiographic conferencing system, currently Blackboard Collaborate. Resources for tutorials are available in our repository of OER for language teachers, LORO, Languages Open Resources Online[1].

---

1. http://loro.open.ac.uk/

2. Aims and objectives

I am reporting here on a small section of a case study I carried out into the professional practices of OU language teachers when engaging with OER. In the case study, data was generated through professional conversation and peer observation of twelve teachers of French and Spanish at the OU as they were preparing a lesson and again reflecting on the lesson afterwards (Beaven, 2013). The data was analysed using applied thematic analysis.

The attributes, skills and knowledge characteristic of distance (language) teaching and student support have been categorised as cognitive (supporting and developing learning through mediating the course and subject content); affective (providing a supportive, committed environment and enhancing the students' self-esteem); and systemic (providing supportive, effective, and student-friendly administrative and ICT systems) (Tait, 2000).

When starting my research, I asked myself to what extent engaging with open resources and practices might necessitate the exercise of the above attributes, skills and knowledge, and whether it was a useful tool in enhancing the professional practices of teachers. The wider research that this chapter is based on also sought to understand whether teachers reuse, adapt and share OER, and whether this engagement with OER might have a positive impact or influence on their practice. Indeed, some of the literature seems to support this view. After the initial emphasis on the creation of OER and OER collections, in the second and current phase of the OER movement the focus is moving from resources to practices, or "using OER in a way that improves learning experiences and [innovative] educational scenarios" (Camilleri, Ehlers, & Pawlowski, 2014, p. 12). As Ehlers (2011) explains, "OER usage, re-usage, sharing and creation are not an end in itself", but engaging with them has to result in better teaching practices and learning experiences (p. 7).

In this chapter, I discuss specific resources used in class by three of the teachers in my study, so as to highlight the tacit professional knowledge that they use when developing or adapting teaching resources.

Chapter 7

3.   What I did

The resources produced or adapted by the teachers in my study are what Weller (2009) calls 'little OER', and are fairly simple in their design. Although they might not seem particularly promising at yielding much of an insight into the professional practices of the teachers that have created or re-versioned them, by discussing them in detail it becomes clear that they represent a considerable body of tacit professional knowledge, as the following vignettes illustrate.

3.1.   Vignette #1: can I exploit, adapt and enlarge the resource?

S1 is an experienced teacher of Spanish at the OU, and he sees his role as being that of a guide through the learning process. The aim of his tutorials is to provide useful language practice that will enable students to use whatever language they have been learning through their distance study materials. When he looks for OER to use in class, he asks himself: "Is that activity going to be useful in terms of communication? Can I exploit it, can I adapt it, can I enlarge it?"

Although he considers that creating one's own resources is an important part of a teacher's role and enjoys the opportunity to be creative, he also acknowledges that time is an issue. However, he considers that creativity in teaching is not just about making new resources, but also about the "performance" in the classroom, the enactment of the lesson with a particular group; in order to avoid merely operating routinely, he injects "an element of creativity" into his lessons, trying out new, different ways of doing things.

Figure 1 is one of the OER for the beginners' Spanish course available through LORO. S1 explained that he had used this resource often in the past and was using it again in the tutorial we were discussing. Although he starts the activity as suggested, to ensure students know the relevant vocabulary, he then deviates from the lesson notes. These notes suggest students describe where an item of furniture is or to ask each other the location of a piece of furniture. S1 explained that in the original activity there is no information gap, and therefore little communicative purpose, so he turned it into a guessing game, which is more interesting and fun for students.

Figure 1. Mi habitación (My room) – lesson notes and screen from LORO

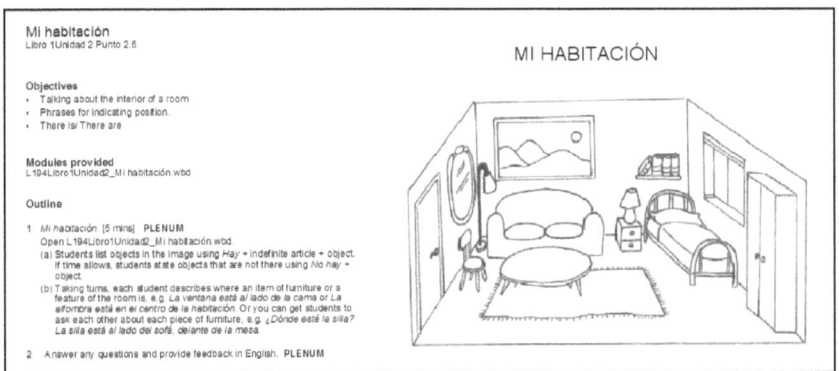

As well as changing the way the main activity worked, S1 devised a follow-up activity about nouns including the sound 'r':

> "Then I did a quick follow-up activity to practice the pronunciation of the sound 'r' with words such as *lámpara, alfombra, armario, puerta, libros* and so on…".

In this vignette, we have seen how S1 exploits, adapts and expands the use of a specific OER in his tutorial.

3.2. Vignette #2: metalanguage and reflection

F1 has taught French at the OU at all levels, including beginners, for over ten years. She believes the main aim of tutorials is to provide students with the opportunity to practise their speaking skills, and this is what she was advised when she joined the OU. However, over the years, she has come to realise that the students need help with study skills:

Chapter 7

> "I feel that my role now is not just to provide opportunities for speaking, but also for developing language learning skills and distance learning skills... And that involves goal setting, self-reflection, evaluation of learning, etc".

F1's tutorial welcome screen is in French, and includes a list of the grammatical structures and vocabulary areas that will be practised in the tutorial (Figure 2). At first, it might seem a bit daunting to students, who might not be familiar with the language or with the meaning of some of these headings.

Figure 2. F1's welcome screen

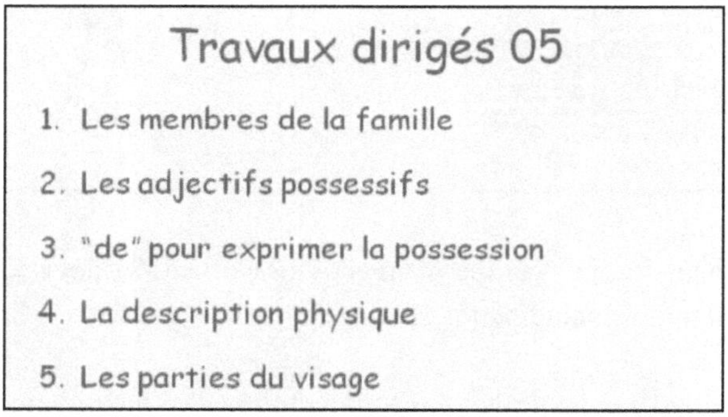

> **Travaux dirigés 05**
> 1. Les membres de la famille
> 2. Les adjectifs possessifs
> 3. "de" pour exprimer la possession
> 4. La description physique
> 5. Les parties du visage

However, as she explained, F1 tries to introduce "very repetitive, very ritualistic" expressions in French in her communications with students from the start via the different systems at her disposal (personal emails, postings on the class forum, feedback on the students' assignments, etc). These might include greetings, farewells, and thanks for participating in activities. She also posts an agenda with the content of the next tutorial in the online forum for her group. She writes this in French, and then includes a translation into English at the end. So when students attend the tutorial, the welcome screen in French is not as daunting, as they have already seen this, and the translation, in the forum message.

When we discussed the possibly daunting use of grammatical terminology in the welcome screen, F1 explained:

"When I used to teach face-to-face [with another institution...], students were begging me to teach them English grammar and I used to joke, "I am qualified to teach you French grammar, but not English grammar". Then I qualified as an ESOL and as an EAP tutor and I did that quite a lot, teaching grammar. I also worked in adult literacy; I qualified as well as an adult literacy tutor and it's all about – [...] "Oh, no, we are not going to bother their pretty heads with all that jargon". It's not about jargon; it's about understanding a structure. It's about being able to memorise because you understand the bigger picture, and it's that dreadful school of thought that did away with grammar teaching at school. It's not about prescriptive grammar, it's about descriptive grammar, it's about understanding, it's about choices. So, when you say "nominal group", it's very important because that's when you are going to understand why you made all these mistakes. It's because of your word order, because the word order is different. So I always give them... not too much, but I make it understandable, I make it accessible, and then it becomes quite obvious".

Figure 3. F1's tutorial evaluation resource

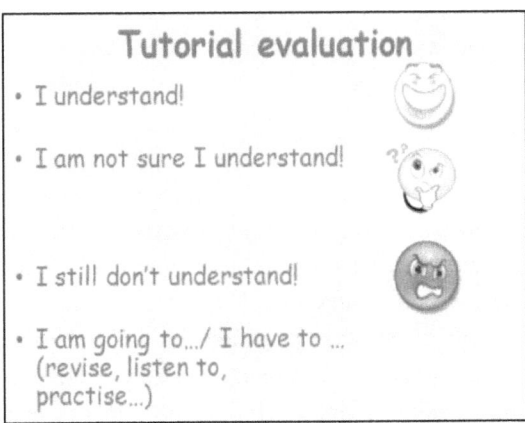

F1 always ends the tutorial with an evaluation (see Figure 3). For her, what is important is not only how students feel they've done, but she also asks them:

Chapter 7

"What are you going to do? What is the next step? [...] It's about becoming a self-reflective learner, and being proactive, and really developing independent learning skills. You need to be able to assess where you are, where you should be at, and what you need to do in order to get there...".

This vignette has shown how this teacher incorporates metalanguage and reflection in the resources she uses, and the professional knowledge and understanding she draws on when doing this.

3.3. Vignette #3: providing a security blanket

S2 is another very experienced teacher of Spanish at the OU. She sees her role in relation to her students as being "a facilitator of their studies, one of the tools in their course of study". She also explains that, with beginner students, at the start of the course she tends to be "more teacher-like, and by the end it's tutor/ facilitator". With more advanced students on other courses, she adopts the role of facilitator from the start.

S2's resource is for an activity to practise telling the time (see Figure 4). This is the second screen of the tutorial, after a welcome screen, and is the first of a sequence of seven screens and activities which start with very controlled practice, and move on to freer practice, as is standard in communicative language teaching.

This screen is a reminder of some of the language that students have already covered in the course. S2 also sends her students a preparation document before the class with the language that is going to be practised in the tutorial. However, she knows that not all students will have time to study the preparation document, so she has modified the original resource by adding the box at the bottom with the time expressions, and the two smaller boxes at the top. This rather didactic approach fits with how she sees her role at the start of the beginners' course. Moreover, the addition of the language boxes with the key linguistic structures also serves the role of providing affective support for students:

"It's really there as a reminder to them rather than having to look at notes or whatever. […] It's quite early on [in the course] so their confidence is not as great in general… That's why I do that, I think it's more like a comfort blanket for them".

Figure 4. S2's adapted resource from LORO for telling the time

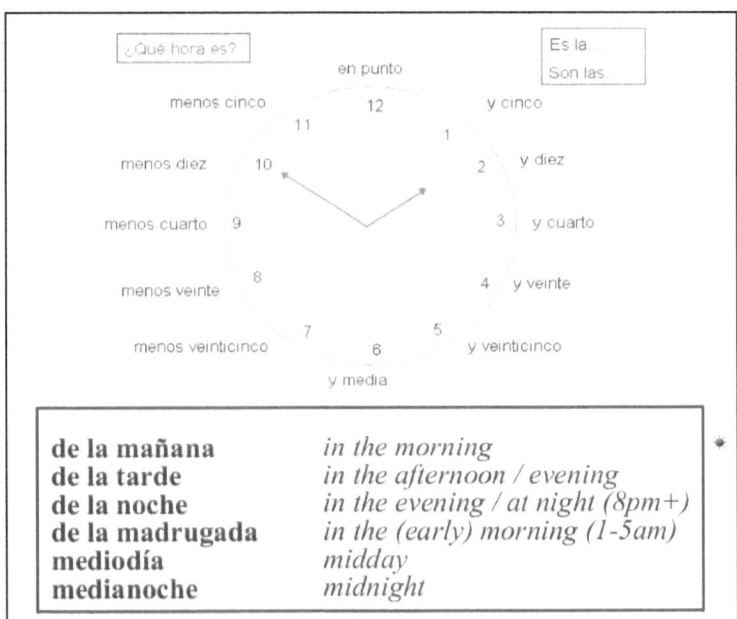

S2 is aware that for students who are new to learning from a distance, online tutorials can be challenging, and that many feel nervous "because it is nerve-racking being online because, although you can't be seen, you can't hide at all, whereas in face-to-face, you can hide [laughs]". So the addition of the language structures to the screen offers students comfort and security. The tutorial, however, is sequenced so that, as students gain confidence with the system, with each other, and with the language they are practising, they also move away from the very controlled, supported practice to more open, freer activities. The final activity is a photo of a young woman in a tracksuit, and

85

Chapter 7

students speculate about her daily routine. This time, though, "they can't rely on the comfort blanket that I've been putting up throughout the tutorial. It's more natural in fact, more real, they don't have their notes and everything in front of them".

4. Discussion

These vignettes illustrate how teachers use and adapt OER, and the sorts of tacit professional knowledge that they make use of when engaging with such resources and practices.

S1's adaptation shows how he uses resources to revise and extend the students' skills in ways that are congruent with his communicative approach, and how he adapts the use of the resource to prevent his own professional obsolescence and inject an element of creativity to his performance in the classroom.

F1's introductory slide can be seen to embody her beliefs about the importance of understanding linguistic and grammatical metalanguage; her final screen represents her interest in students developing self-reflection and independent learning skills.

S2's case illustrates how the additions the tutor makes to the resource fit with her self-image as a teacher. By adding text boxes, her communicative approach moves students on from controlled to freer practice, and shows her understanding of the importance of affective support for students in an online environment.

5. Conclusion

The three vignettes I have presented illustrate how, when engaging with OER, the teachers in my study draw on their tacit professional knowledge, which includes cognitive, affective and systemic attributes, skills and knowledge.

As Petrides et al. (2010) point out, "OER—as resources that lend themselves to collaboration, knowledge sharing about practices, adaptation and reuse—support conversations and practices that may not traditionally be available through professional development" (p. 383). If the aim of engaging with open educational resources and practices is that this results in better teaching practices and learning experiences (Ehlers, 2011), then it is important to find ways and spaces where teachers can articulate and share their tacit knowledge when engaging with OER, so that it can become "commonly usable knowledge" that will enhance the quality of teaching and learning (Iiyoshi & Kumar, 2008, p. 436).

References

Beaven, T. (2013). Use and reuse of OER: Professional conversations with language teachers. *Journal of e-Learning and Knowledge Society, 9*(1) 59-71. Retrieved from http://oro.open.ac.uk/36500/

Camilleri, A. F., Ehlers, U. D., & Pawlowski, J. (2014). *State of the art review of quality issues related to open educational resources (OER)*. Luxembourg. Retrieved from http://www.pedocs.de/volltexte/2014/9101/pdf/European_Commission_2014_OER.pdf

Ehlers, U.-D. (2011). From open educational resources to open educational practices. *eLearning Papers, 23*(March), 1-8. Retrieved from http://www.openeducationeuropa.eu/en/download/file/fid/22240

Iiyoshi, T., & Kumar, M. S. V. (Eds). (2008). *Opening up education - The collective advancement of education through open technology, open content, and open knowledge.* Cambridge, Massachusetts: MIT Press. Retrieved from https://mitpress.mit.edu/sites/default/files/titles/content/9780262515016_Open_Access_Edition.pdf

Petrides, L., Jimes, C., Middleton-Detzner, C., & Howell, H. (2010). OER as a model for enhanced teaching and learning. In Proceedings of *Barcelona Open Ed 2010, The Seventh Annual Open Education Conference November 2-4 2010* (pp. 379-388). Barcelona: Universitat Oberta de Catalunya. Retrieved from http://www.icde.org/filestore/Resources/Handbooks/ProceedingsOpenEd2010.pdf

Smith, M. S., & Casserly, C. M. (2006). The promise of open educational resources. *Change: The Magazine of Higher Learning, 38*(5), 8-17. doi:10.3200/CHNG.38.5.8-17

Tait, A. (2000). Planning student support for open and distance learning. *Open Learning: The Journal of Open and Distance Learning, 15*(3), 287-299. Retrieved from http://www.tandfonline.com/doi/abs/10.1080/713688410#.VBWiFpRdVQA

Weller, M. (2009, December 9). Big OER and little OER. *The Ed Techie blog*. Retrieved from http://goo.gl/XVJ94o

8. Dyslexia in modern language learning: A case study on collaborative task-design for inclusive teaching and learning in an online context

Anna Motzo[1] and Debora Quattrocchi[2]

Abstract

In recent years, universities have been involved in developing new strategies to promote widening participation in higher education, and consequently they have been focusing on increasing the variety of support offered to students with disabilities for a more inclusive and widely accessible learning environment. However, there is a common feeling amongst practitioners and learners that learning disabilities are harder to recognise than physical disabilities, and therefore less prioritised. Such is still the case with dyslexia, a learning difference (term chosen here by the authors to describe a difficulty in the cognitive processing of information), which unlike most physical disabilities, is not always identified and therefore addressed with appropriate dyslexia-friendly learning materials and approaches. Furthermore, the staggering growth in the use of Information and Communication Technology (ICT) in education raises questions about how the new technologies can support an inclusive learning approach. This case study provides an outline of the Dyslexia in Modern Language Learning (DMLL) collaborative project, aimed at bridging the gap between language learning and learning differences (specifically dyslexia) in an online distance learning framework.

Keywords: dyslexia, e-learning, OER, OEP, modern languages, inclusive teaching.

---

1. The Open University, United Kingdom; a.motzo@open.ac.uk.

2. The Open University in London, United Kingdom; d.quattrocchi@open.ac.uk.

How to cite this chapter: Motzo, A., & Quattrocchi, D. (2015). Dyslexia in modern language learning: A case study on collaborative task-design for inclusive teaching and learning in an online context. In K. Borthwick, E. Corradini, & A. Dickens (Eds), *10 years of the LLAS elearning symposium: Case studies in good practice* (pp. 89-102). Dublin: Research-publishing.net. doi:10.14705/rpnet.2015.000270

Chapter 8

1. Context/rationale

The Open University (OU) provides high-quality distance learning courses on a wide range of subjects to adult (16+) learners. OU courses usually run online and involve, depending on the course, a combination of both synchronous (teleconference, face to face tutorials) and asynchronous (forums, wikis, blogs) activities.

Given the particular nature of these online courses in open learning settings, learners must be able to work autonomously, in a self-paced way and the tutor acts predominantly as a facilitator.

As a result, online courses can be particularly challenging for students with learning differences. According to the British Dyslexia Institute[1], between 4% and 10% of the UK population is affected by dyslexia, a learning difference which affects the cognitive processes in written and spoken language. Furthermore, Higher Education Statistics Agency (HESA) figures for 2005/6 revealed that 2.6% of the total higher education population is dyslexic[2]. In light of this, the OU has put in place a support network to provide standard guidance to students with disabilities and learning difficulties and offers a range of resources such as learning materials in accessible/alternative formats, guidance on how to develop effective study skills and the opportunity for extra one to one tutorials. General guidance for tutors is also available.

The OU's language portfolio includes seven languages, taught at different levels and in a blended context which uses a combination of online and face to face settings. The learning materials are produced in-house and comprise a variety of formats such as print and online interactive materials. Both the production and the presentation of the materials are equally crucial: tutorials are designed and delivered with an inclusive teaching approach, to encompass a variety of learning styles, preferences and differences.

---

1. http://www.dyslexia-inst.org.uk

2. http://www2.le.ac.uk/offices/ssds/accessability/staff/supporting-students-with-dyslexia/dyslexia_guidelines/dyslexia_he

The Department of Languages is keen to address issues related to disability and learning differences and tutors have been working with disability advisers for years. However, it was felt that tutors needed more specific support and guidance to allow them to provide sensitive and effective assistance to students with learning differences in their subject-areas.

It was in light of this, that in 2013 the OU Department of Languages set up the DMLL project to bridge the gap between language learning and learning difficulties in an online distance learning framework. Twelve language tutors from different regions joined the seven-month project and worked collaboratively to build up a knowledge bank, through the sharing of good practice, reflection and peer feedback.

2. Aims and objectives

The project's main purposes were to create a repository of knowledge on the topic of dyslexia and language teaching/learning, a set of guidelines for language tutors, academic and advisory staff and produce dyslexia-friendly Open Educational Resources (OERs). In this case study, we (as project participants) would like to illustrate how the group worked collaboratively on planning and implementing new task-design for inclusive teaching and learning in an online context. We have identified and worked through the followings aims and objectives:

Aims:

- to investigate the main pedagogical implications of dyslexics learning a language in an online context;

- to address the current shortage of open access dyslexia-friendly teaching and learning language resources;

- to improve the development of task-design for inclusive teaching and learning in an online context.

Chapter 8

Objectives:

- to share findings about the existing relevant literature;

- to provide examples of the use of new technologies to develop inclusive transferable task-design;

- to present examples of an inclusive task-design framework produced collaboratively in light of Open Educational Practices (OEPs).

3. What we did

The project consisted of three phases:

- phase 1: collaborative creation of a bank of knowledge and a repository for the open educational resources, length: seven weeks;

- phase 2: collaborative creation of the "Guide to Good Practice" toolkit, length: three months;

- phase 3: dissemination: ongoing.

A workspace for the DMLL workgroup was set up, which included a platform (*OU Live*) for synchronous online meeting used for the plenary sessions, a forum tool for asynchronous discussion, and a repository for uploading the work produced.

3.1. Phase 1

The first phase of the project consisted of four online meetings, the first of which was a briefing. In the briefing, participants were divided into three teams of four and were asked to familiarise themselves with existing OU resources for dyslexic students and to evaluate their usefulness, in order to build up some background knowledge on the topic of dyslexia and language learning and identify key issues in the literature studied. Teams were encouraged to continue the discussion in the forum. In subsequent meetings, participants were asked to prepare a set of guidelines for lesson planning and delivery based on the key issues identified in their research and ultimately to produce open online teaching resources to upload to the OU's repository: Languages Open Resources Online (LORO[1]).

The collaborative work took place via online meetings held roughly every three weeks on *OU Live*, the OU's teleconference platform and as such an ideal tool for discussion of key issues and immediate sharing of ideas and feedback. Between meetings, communication and collaboration between teams (or team members) took place via email and predominantly via the asynchronous forum specifically set up for the project. Although each team exchanged messages on the forum specific to their work and clearly labelled with the team name, the whole group had access to all posts and this meant that there was maximal sharing of findings and ideas between all participants, including the project leaders. All materials, including academic literature, bibliography, guidelines and newly created resources were stored in the project repository, accessible to all participants.

The structure of each meeting (with the exception of the initial briefing) was similar, including standing items such as presentation of and discussion about key findings on designated areas of work, showcasing of resources, peer feedback, evaluation and next steps.

All tasks were designed by individuals and shared first with the team for initial feedback and revision; they were subsequently showcased to the whole group for further feedback. Tutors tested their resources with both dyslexic and non-dyslexic students, thus creating opportunities for improvement and reflection. Following final feedback, the tasks were polished, converted into whiteboard (wbd) format in order to be viewed on *OU Live* and uploaded to LORO, tagged as 'Dyslexia friendly resources'.

---

[1]. http://loro.open.ac.uk

3.2. Phase 2

The second phase of the project consisted of two meetings; the main task was contributing to the creation of the 'Guide to Good Practice' toolkit, aimed at language tutors, learning support teams and academic teams. Individual or team's contributions to the guide were posted on a designated wiki arranged by relevant topics. In this phase the emphasis was on reflection and evaluation. Activities also included tandem teaching and peer observations. Online tutorials were recorded with students' permission. Tandem teaching and peer observations were also followed up by 'reflective activity evaluation logs', and stored in the project repository and accessible to all participants.

3.3. Phase 3

Finally, participants engaged in a programme of dissemination activities, organised both internally, as OU staff development events, and outside the OU, as workshops for teachers in schools in collaboration with the Routes into Languages project[1].

4. Discussion

4.1. Key findings and their implications in task-design in an online classroom

From the project we gained a better understanding of how the dyslexic brain processes information. The right hemisphere, responsible for creativity, is more developed in dyslexic people than the left hemisphere, responsible for acquiring language. The main implications in language teaching and learning are that dyslexic students prefer learning in multidimensional images, have a holistic rather than a sequential approach, and are more creative than analytical thinkers. In language learning, dyslexic students may encounter difficulties in the

---

1. www.routesintolanguages.ac.uk

following areas: understanding sounds correctly, retaining vocabulary, spelling and reading, sequencing thoughts and structuring sentences. They often muddle polysyllabic words (Crombie, 2000).

In light of this, the DMLL group felt that the production of learning materials, as an essential aspect of successful teaching in an online environment, should address these differences and that activities should be designed to reflect a variety of learning styles. It also pinpointed the following tenets of inclusive task-design should:

- be based on a Multisensory Structured Language (MSL) approach: a combination of learning tools (such as colour coding, mind-mapping, etc.) and stimuli through two or more sensory channels (hearing, saying, feeling, seeing);

- include clear learning objectives, break activities into scaffolded steps, provide opportunities for active and discovery learning, with some elements of explicit teaching and over-learning;

- make the most of the potential for inclusivity offered by the online tools.

OU Live offers a variety of tools (drag and drop, chat box, multiple speaker, polling options, emoticons and pointers) to facilitate the deployment of kinaesthetic, multisensory and interactive elements in the online classroom, and it therefore appeals to learners with different learning styles. The wbd resources, used during the online tutorials, allow a high degree of interaction and personalisation as users can easily manipulate the style of content (e.g. colour, font, size) according to their individual needs and preferences. Furthermore, the online sessions can be recorded and reach those students who cannot attend live, need repetition for consolidation of learning, or work at a different pace. Besides, students can save the learning materials created for/during the tutorials and reuse them online outside the classroom for further autonomous practice encouraging peer-to-peer collaboration.

Chapter 8

4.2. Mapping our findings to task-design

The following examples illustrate in practice how we used specific technology in inclusive task-design for an online setting; how we addressed student needs and prepared the right learning environment when designing or adapting educational resources.

4.2.1. Example of an auditory discrimination activity using visual and oral stimuli

Auditory discrimination problems result in the inability of the brain to organise and make sense of the sounds of a language, which leads to a misinterpretation of sounds. This can be impeding in language learning. However, many people think through images, and teaching can address this by adopting a MSL approach.

The extracts of the example below are part of a whole activity designed for a Level 1 German beginners' course. The activity carried out in an online tutorial can be broken into smaller units according to student needs and was designed to introduce four sounds in German: [ei], [ie], [eu] and [au]. Each sound is colour-coded in order to be recognisable when embedded within other sounds (words) (Figure 1).

Figure 1. The use of colour-coding aid in sound discrimination

ei - ie - au - eu

The example below focuses on the sound [ie].

The aim of the activity is for students to learn to distinguish the sound [ie] by linking the sound to images representing that sound in English and the corresponding sound in German. In Figure 2, step 1, the tutor introduces the sound [ie] orally and visually anchoring it to the visual 'Bee' (which is pronounced as the –ie in German). Subsequently, the phoneme, which was hidden behind the box in the previous step, is shown graphically (grapheme) as the tutor removes the rectangular box as displayed in step 2.

Figure 2. Anchoring a sound to a visual aid

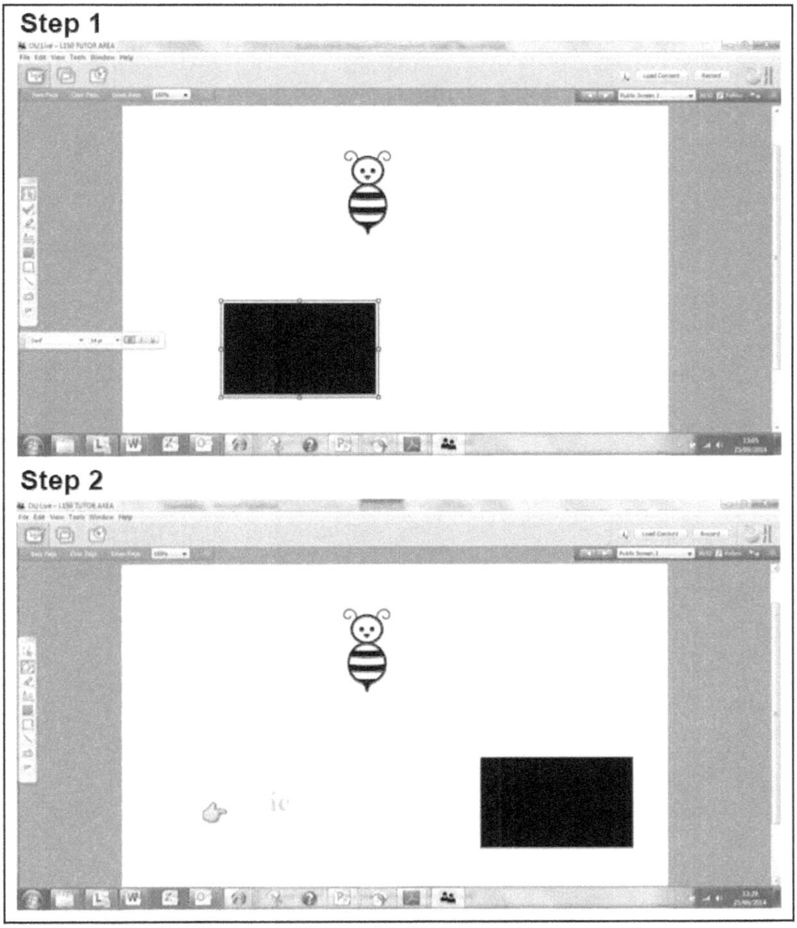

In step 3 of Figure 3, the tutor reinforces the sound recognition by using a mnemonic aid (Chief Bee). This is particularly useful to dyslexic students who

Chapter 8

experience poor visual and auditory mnemonic retention and benefit from special strategies to reinforce memory mechanisms. Subsequently in step 4, students are exposed to a range of words containing the same phoneme and are invited to practise both in written form and by saying the listed words.

Figure 3. A mnemonic aid to reinforce sound recognition

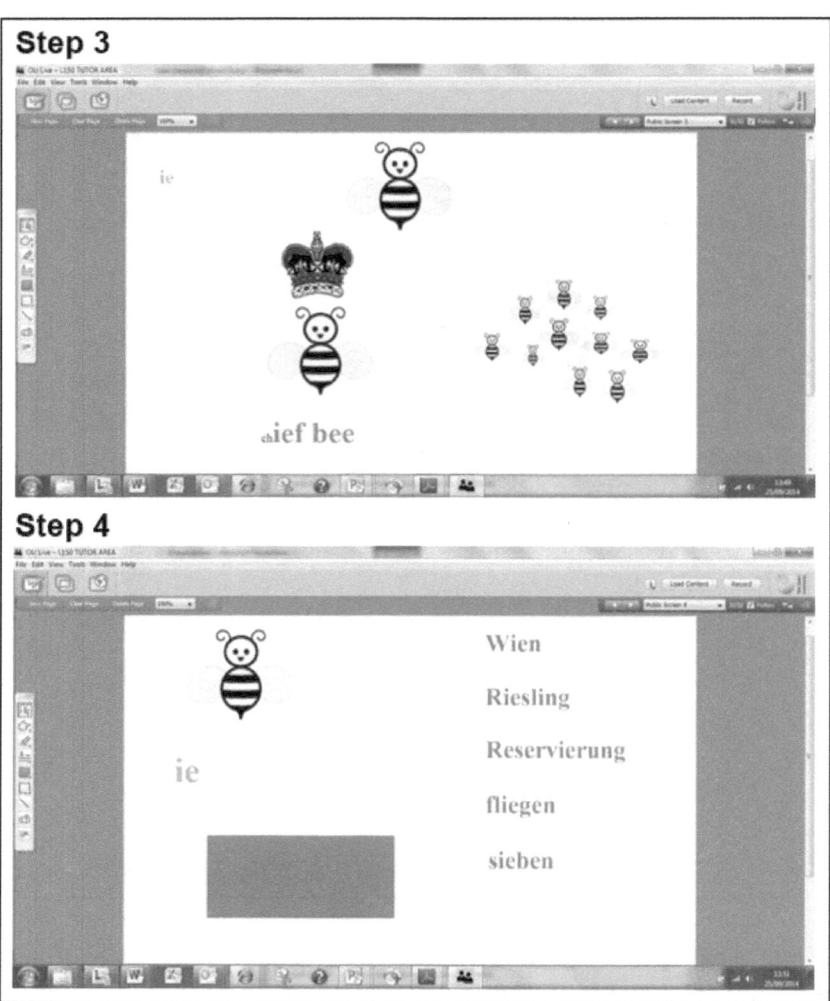

The activity develops in further stages in which all the remaining sounds are introduced and eventually students are asked to take part in an interactive activity in which they have to practise sound discrimination by using a polling tool available. The phonemes for the designated sounds are colour coded. As they hear the new word, students are asked to press the corresponding letter link showed on the left side of the screen and here replicated on the whiteboard (Figure 4). Variations to this task can be offered if the tutor perceives that the additional link of pressing letters for specific sounds may be too complicated for certain students and they could advise students to use the pointers to show which sound is being produced.

Figure 4. A polling tool to practise sound recognition

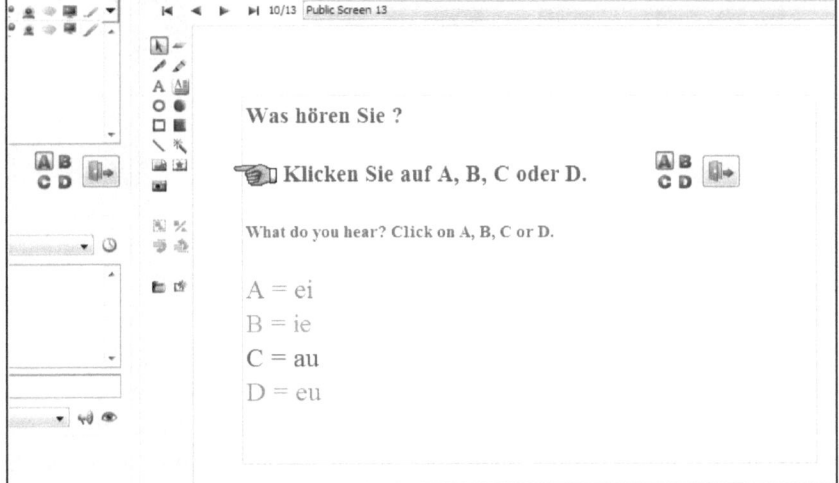

4.2.2. Example of a kinaesthetic multisensory activity

In this second example, the whiteboard slide in Figure 5 is part of a set of slides used in an Italian beginners' course. The slide can be used on its own to prompt students to talk about free time activities or as part of a set of activities on talking about the time and expressing frequency. This is an interactive,

Chapter 8

collaborative activity. Students are asked to match the phrases scattered around the whiteboard with the correct image. In turn, students practise their oral skills by producing a sentence using the clues provided and the tutor will check the correct pronunciation.

Figure 5. Interactive collaborative tools (drag and drop and pointers)

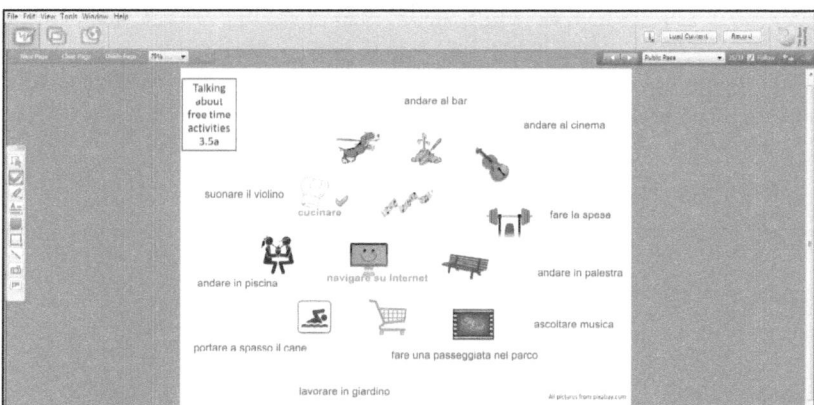

This online activity, due to its versatility in making an image-text association is effective with all types of learners, particularly in a beginners' class. Therefore, it was felt potentially appropriate for dyslexic learners too as they perform well in practical activities and tend to think through images. They also perform better if involved in kinaesthetic multisensory tasks which encourage a holistic rather than sequential approach. Nevertheless, some amendments from the original version were required in order to make it fully dyslexia-friendly. To address the dyslexic learners, we reduced the amount of text and images on each slide, used a sans-serif font and an off-white background. In the online setting, students collaboratively carry out the activity of labelling the images by dragging and dropping the text on the right place and by progressively changing the colour of each correct label from blue to red (or any suitable colour). Pointers can also be used by the tutor to confirm the correctness of the activity (see below the green tick next to the image of a chef hat labelled as '*cucinare*') or by the students to point the activities they want to describe.

Both resources offer an opportunity to see how to use kinaesthetic elements and a variety of stimuli (oral, written, visual) to facilitate different learning styles and how to break down activities into achievable steps to enhance learners' autonomy[1].

5. Conclusion

The DMLL project set out to provide an opportunity for participants to work collaboratively and identify the main barriers that students with dyslexia (and other learning difficulties) face in language learning. It also aimed to encourage the tutors involved to reflect on their own teaching practice and rethink how inclusivity can be pragmatically addressed in online language teaching. Consequently, it raised questions about how to plan and implement effective task-design for an inclusive online teaching and learning. Finally and most importantly, the project outcomes and the resources (such as teaching guidelines, lesson plans and materials) were shared with other practitioners in a spirit of open educational practice.

The examples presented here provide some useful insights into how to exploit the potential of the online environment to create interactive and engaging resources targeted primarily at dyslexic learners but suitable for all.

Reference

Crombie, M. A. (2000). Dyslexia and the Learning of a foreign language in school: Where are we going? *Dyslexia, 6*(2), 112-123.

---

1. Overall, dyslexic students found the MSL and the visual mnemonic aids used in the classroom extremely useful, particularly to disentangle the sound-spelling combination. Non-dyslexic students found the materials engaging and welcomed the stronger connection between images and physical sensory activities.

Chapter 8

Further readings

Crombie, M. A. (2003). *Dyslexia and modern foreign languages: Gaining success in an inclusive context*. David Fulton Publishers Ltd. Retrieved from http://goo.gl/6bMWsT

Gallardo, M., Heiser, H., Arias-McLaughlin, X., & Fayram, J. (2013). *Supporting students with dyslexia in distance modern language studies. A guide to good practice*. Retrieved from http://loro.open.ac.uk/3912/

Habib, L., & al. (2012). Dyslexic students in higher education and virtual learning environments: An exploratory study. *Journal of Computer Assisted Learning, 28*(6), 574-584. doi:10.1111/j.1365-2729.2012.00486.x

Hill, J., & Roed, J. (2005). *A survey of the ways universities cope with the needs of dyslexic foreign language learners and, in consultation with tutors and learners, the piloting of appropriate assessment methods*. LLAS. Retrieved from https://www.heacademy.ac.uk/sites/default/files/sussex.pdf

Nijakowska, J. (2010). *Dyslexia in the foreign language classroom*. Bristol: Multilingual Matters.

Schneider, E., & Crombie, M. A. (2003). *Dyslexia and language learning*. Milton Park: David Fulton Publishers.

Silipo, S. (n.d.). *Kinaesthetic activity, dyslexia-friendly*. Retrieved from http://loro.open.ac.uk/4203/

Vilar Beltrán, E., Abbott, C., & Jones, J. (2013). *Inclusive language education and digital technology*. Bristol: Multilingual Matters.

Winchester, S. (2013). *German diphthongs, dyslexia-friendly*. Retrieved from http://loro.open.ac.uk/3353/

Section 3.
Fostering creativity in the classroom

9 Reflections on a personal journey in learning design

Julie Watson[1]

1. How did you become interested in using technology in your professional life?

My personal and professional interest in technology dates back to Rome and the 1980s. I was working as an English teacher at the *Istituto Britannico* in Via Quattro Fontane, nearby to our English language teaching competitor, the British Council. Both schools were confusingly known as *il British* and I was a regular visitor to the Council's lending library and its rather ancient book collection. During that time the library became the proud owners of several brand new, imposing BBC Micros developed by Acorn Computers (see Figure 1). Accompanied by a seriously off-putting set of user manuals and some very floppy disks, nobody quite knew what to do with them. I began exploring in an attempt to learn something about what computers could do. One day I was approached by the Chief Librarian. The librarian on the main desk had informed him that I was a computer 'expert'. I was sole claimant for this title as no-one else had got beyond locating the on/off switch! He offered me a financial incentive to create an introductory program for library visitors using the Acorn Basic programming language, an opportunity which I seized. And thus was launched a new direction in my career, setting me firmly on the path towards elearning. Later, in the early 1990s, I wrote my Masters dissertation in the area of 'email literacy', becoming further immersed in the field, and then, in 2001, was appointed to lead a team of EAP teacher-developers from a six-university consortium in the now generally-forgotten UK E-Universities (UKEU) project. Our mission was to create and deliver an online EAP course as part of an initiative to put UK university degree

---

1. University of Southampton, Southampton, United Kingdom; J.Watson@soton.ac.uk.

How to cite this chapter: Watson, J. (2015). Reflections on a personal journey in learning design. In K. Borthwick, E. Corradini, & A. Dickens (Eds), *10 years of the LLAS elearning symposium: Case studies in good practice* (pp. 105-115). Dublin: Research-publishing. net. doi:10.14705/rpnet.2015.000271

programmes online for students across the world, a slightly surreal experience to look back on, given where we are now! Ten years ago, I presented this project and my first tentative thoughts about learning design at the very first LLAS elearning symposium.

Figure 1. A BBC micro computer[1]

2. How has your use and knowledge of technology in language learning and teaching developed over time?

In 2001, I began using learning object technology for elearning. Any creative technology available tended to cost a lot or be designed for other purposes, and there were no free web 2.0 tools. *DreamWeaver*, a commercial software

---

1. Sdource: Magnus Lien, Norsk Teknisk Museum/commons.wikimedia.org

program designed for creating web pages, became my first learning object 'authoring' tool, with a bit of customisation. Designing for online learning was a blank canvas, so I based my first learning design for learning objects on a blend of, what seemed to me, pertinent aspects (for the online environment) of good practice in Communicative Language Teaching (CLT), and design features distilled from emerging research findings about how users interacted with the internet and its content. Though I felt lost, in retrospect I think I was in some ways in a fortunate position. I couldn't be distracted by a huge array of technologies with unexplored potential for educational purposes. I wasn't in danger of being in love with technology for its own sake. In fact, I was usually in a state of disappointment because of what I couldn't achieve with what I did have! That was a long time ago and things are different now.

In my professional life today as an online course and resource designer and developer I frequently feel I need to catch up. I try to experiment creatively with new web technologies, many of which are not designed for education but reflect creative and exciting possibilities for engaging students and aiding effective learning online. Although learning objects are, surprisingly, still around, the elearning scene now feels a bit like Christmas, a sort of technology gift season. By mixing and matching other technologies in my elearning development work, I think I have been able to meet students' needs more effectively. The research and expanding literature in the field also means it's much easier to know what other work is being done, even though I sometimes feel that I have now exchanged an elearning desert for a jungle!

3. How has contact with colleagues impacted on the way you use technology in language learning and teaching?

The commercial online language learning products that I have designed and developed (e.g. EAP Toolkit, a free-standing online resource set to help international students develop their English for Academic Purposes and study skills) and open resources (e.g. Prepare for Success –a website of learning

Chapter 9

resources for international students coming to study in the UK; and more recently, the Digital Literacies Toolkit) were all piloted with teaching colleagues and students before being launched. Their role cannot be understated. Contact with colleagues has always helped shape the way the design of technologies evolves or how they are implemented in teaching and learning. I regularly survey licencing institutions and teachers using our toolkits to inform the technology refreshment phases that we carry out periodically. Similarly, student and teacher feedback on the Prepare for Success website has been vital in making important decisions such as when to change from Flash-based activities to HTML5 due to increased access from non-Flash supporting mobile technologies. This website will have surpassed an unimaginable one million visits when you read this! Another recent site enhancement arising from student feedback is the introduction of a blog combined with a 'question wall' to provide an interactive channel of communication with international student users of the website. Contact with colleagues at conferences has also been useful in keeping the ideas flowing and seeding new experiments.

4. How do you use technology in your professional practice now?

I frequently use technology in my professional practice when teaching face-to-face or online. Drawing from an ever-changing range, I use technologies experimentally and rather eclectically. In designing an online course, for example, I try to choose technologies according to the functionalities I need for the learning design to create the best opportunities for learning. The technology doesn't work in isolation but as an aid to the learning task. Perhaps this is a rather obvious statement but it is still easy to make the mistake of choosing the technology before the pedagogy. I have no favourite technology but factors such as simplicity of use, capacity to engage users, and accessibility are important in making the final choice. If the technology is being chosen to facilitate online communication activity, it's important that it is also accessible to an international audience anywhere. This limits the use of some western social media networks such as Facebook and YouTube.

5. How does your knowledge and experience in social media and web 2.0 technologies impact on your professional and teaching life?

5.1. Starting out on the learning design journey: the learning object

Learning design for me began with the internal design of a learning object. In 2002, while leading a team of teachers developing learning objects –the building blocks of the online courses we were creating–, I needed to ensure consistency of the team's output. This entailed recognising and sharing –at the micro level of the learning resource itself– a set of pedagogic features that could be used to package topics and facilitate learning by students using them independently online and interacting with learning object content in different ways. From those learning objects in aspects of EAP and language skill development that I began creating with *DreamWeaver*, a number of common features emerged, reflecting CLT approaches as well as concerns highlighted in the literature of the time by early leaders in the field. The explicit pedagogic features that came to be integral to the design of my learning objects were:

- having a clearly identified learning objective or learning point, reflecting self-containedness (referred to by Koper, Pannekeet, Hendriks, & Hummel, 2004 as 'encapsulation');

- centred on learning activities so that users 'actively' exploit the resources ('learning by doing' Race, 2005);

- personalised learning activities to ensure familiar/meaningful contexts for the student user;

- engaging the user in reflection as well as activity;

- incorporating 2-3 activities that build on each other and unpack more complex learning into discrete learning steps;

- enhancement with useful feedback (explanation as well as answers) and independent resources (e.g. transcript);

- combining multi-media, e.g. text, audio/video links, web links, images to provide variety and accommodate different learning approaches.

Certain technical attributes were being widely recognised as desirable for learning objects especially for enabling their reuse. Much attention was focussed on these technical aspects initially but fortunately, practitioners such as Wiley (2001) highlighted the need for pedagogic attributes as well.

Reusable Learning Objects (RLOs), as they came to be known, were considered more useful if they reflected consistency in size (granularity) and this could be approached through the pedagogic route of estimating learner time needed for activities. The learning object came to be seen as a small unit of learning with generic possibilities rather than a module or course-sized unit. Accessibility and later tagging of learning objects with metadata to allow their discoverability were also seen as desirable. Such concerns and the technological developments they gave rise to paved the way for Open Educational Resources (OER) and searchable teaching and learning repositories. The aggregation of smaller sized learning objects could facilitate online course or module creation, and conversely, the disaggregation of component parts of learning objects –at the simplest level of the media-packaged resource base for an activity– could provide the starting point for a new or repurposed learning object. As my own bank of learning objects grew, it became apparent to me how other elements of a Learning Object could offer scope for repurposing, for example, instructional scaffolding and generic activity types. Sustaining a high level of reuse was (and still is) essential in justifying the significant cost and resource dedication needed to initiate development of online learning resources and courses.

5.2. Learning design for an authoring tool for teachers: LOC

The need for an 'explicit learning design' (Watson, 2010) that could be easily recognised and explained also became central in the development of two commercial products: the EAP and Study Skills Toolkits. In particular, the EAP Toolkit for international students was being licenced by a growing number of UK higher education institutions[1]. Increasingly, institutions licencing these products and teachers integrating them on taught courses were providing feedback on their use and asking if additional learning resources were available. Concurrent with this, in a 2006 joint initiative with the LLAS (Languages Linguistics and Areas Studies) Subject Centre, I had begun to design and develop a learning object authoring tool for teachers (Watson, Dickens, & Gilchrist, 2008). Incorporating the learning design that I created for learning objects, the online LOC tool, as it came to be known, has continued to be adopted by a growing community of teachers to plan, build and publish their own online learning resources supported by a tried and tested pedagogy[2]. Among toolkit-licencing institutions, there are several in which teams of teachers create their own desired toolkit add-ons using the LOC Tool. Perhaps uniquely among authoring tools, the free LOC tool is accompanied by a training workshop in which teachers, new to creating online resources, are not only familiarised with the technical affordances of the LOC tool but, more importantly, through planning, peer engagement and revision, are introduced to good practice in creating effective online resources for their own teaching and learning contexts. To my mind, having an explicit learning design reflected in learning resources (or in an authoring tool for teachers) can help ensure that the learning aim remains the driver in the pedagogy-technology partnership.

5.3. Design at the macro level of the online course

At the macro level of the online course I was also preoccupied with learning design. How could learning objects, used as course building blocks, work effectively with conventional tools such as VLE discussion forums and in the dynamic context of a student learning community and an online teacher? I began developing a model showing how these elements might be integrated to work

---

1. EAP Toolkit for international students www.elanguages.ac.uk/eap_toolkit.php
2. The LOC Tool https://www.llas.ac.uk/projects/2770

together, drawing on the core components (discussion, adaptation, interaction and reflection) and interrelationships of Laurillard's (2002) Conversational Framework for teaching and learning in higher education. This dialogic model also sought to take into account the increasing role of new technologies in the teaching and learning process. I had earlier tried to include some of Laurillard's principles in the internal design of learning objects. I later argued that at the macro level of a course with an online learning community, the inclusion of VLE communication tools and an online tutor with the learning objects could help realise all aspects of the iterative process described in Laurillard's dialogic framework, including the 'reflection' initiated through 'interaction' with the learning objects and continued through a process of ongoing 'adaptation' in learner conceptual understanding, facilitated through peer and teacher 'interaction' in 'discussion' tasks which focus on concepts overarching the topics of the learning objects (Watson, 2010).

From a simple four part model involving the student learning community, learning objects, discussion forum and online tutor, other more complex learning designs took shape. The learning design for the University of Southampton's online MA programme in English Language Teaching is based in a dialogic-based framework in which the discussion forums are "a means to building up and maintaining an e-learning community" (Baker & Watson, 2014, p. 4). Figure 2 (below) shows how learning objects (LOs) link to other elements in a course with similar design, an online pre-sessional course.

Over time, other online courses evolved and gave rise to permutations of the learning design as the repertoire of tools and technologies expanded and their roles and interrelationships changed. For example, when free-standing podcasts (Salmon, Nie, & Edirisingha, 2007) first entered the online learning arena as an educational resource, I experimented with them in various roles (e.g. delivering teacher scaffolding and online 'presence'; or student-created learning resources). More recently, a range of emerging web 2.0 technologies (e.g. video capture tools; virtual curation tools) have filled specific niches within increasingly complex macro learning designs. For example, I have found virtual pinboards or social walls (e.g. Linoit; Padlet) to be more effective tools than discussion forums for ice-breaking or the initial socialisation of students in a range of online courses.

Figure 2. Learning design of an online pre-sessional course

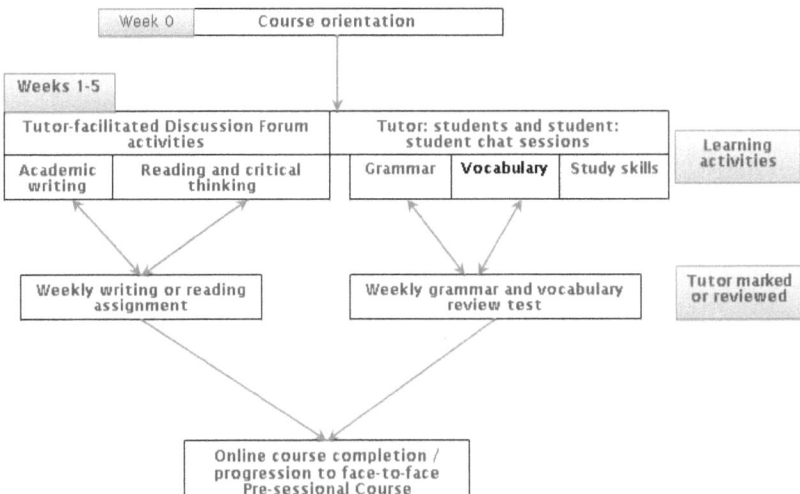

A course I created, which has grown in size and subsequently changed in learning design is 'Get Ready for Southampton'. In the summer of 2014, it was delivered to an online community of 2500 prospective University of Southampton international students[1]. This pre-arrival online distance learning course focuses on English language development and transition to UK academic culture and started in 2005 with a few tutored groups of 25 students, growing by 2013 into a single open student-driven course with over 2500 participants. The connectivist dynamic is now the focal point of the course as evidenced this year by 460 student messages on the Social Wall, 16750 posts across 240 student-created topic threads in the discussion forum, and an incalculable number of student interactions off-course facilitated though in-course exchange of their social media contact details. The online tutor's

1. www.elanguages.ac.uk/get_ready_for_southampton.php

role has become a marginal one and, interestingly, the course reflects a number of the emerging aspects of MOOC pedagogy as identified by Bayne and Ross (2014) and in Watson (2014). The evolution of this online course between 2005 and the present has demonstrated for me not only how a learning design impacts on the course dynamic but also how the course dynamic can impact on the learning design. The older technology of learning objects still has a role in these courses albeit this role has changed and is changing in relation to each course's learning design.

Interestingly, Anderson and Dron (2011) investigating different 'generations' of distance education pedagogy (cognitive-behaviourist, social constructivist and connectivist), found that the learning designs of high quality distance education reflect features of all three past and present generations, and in this way provide "a well-rounded educational experience" (p. 8). This view is further supported by Bayne and Ross (2014), who recently noted that MOOCs are increasingly complex, reflecting "multiple pedagogic forms and intentions" with the cMOOC/xMOOC binary "no longer representative or particularly useful" for understanding the learning design of online courses (p. 8).

My personal journey in learning design has been one with many twists and turns along the way in response to both technological change and awareness of a need to adapt for the individual circumstances of each course, but I hope it has also been one that has always had the aim of enhancing the student learning experience at the heart of it.

References

Anderson T., & Dron, J. (2011). Three generations of distance learning education pedagogy. *International Review of Research in Open and Distance Learning, 12*(3). Retrieved from http://www.irrodl.org/index.php/irrodl/article/view/890/1663

Baker, W., & Watson, J. (2014). Mastering the online master's: Developing and delivering an online MA in English language teaching through a dialogic-based framework. *Innovations in Education and Teaching International, 51*(5), 483-496. doi:10.1080/14703297.2013.796712

Bayne, S., & Ross, J. (2014). *The pedagogy of the massive open online course (MOOC): The UK view*. Edinburgh: THE Higher Education Academy. Retrieved from https://www.heacademy.ac.uk/sites/default/files/HEA_Edinburgh_MOOC_WEB_240314_1.pdf

Koper, R., Pannekeet, K., Hendriks, M., & Hummel, H. (2004). Building communities for the exchange of learning objects: theoretical foundations and requirements. *ALT-J, Research in Learning Technology, 12*(1), 21-35. doi:10.1080/0968776042000211502

Laurillard, D. (2002). *Rethinking university teaching: A framework for the effective use of learning technologies* (2nd ed.). London: Routledge Falmer.

Race, P. (2005). 500 tips for open and online learning (2nd ed). London: RoutledgeFalmer.

Salmon, G. K., Nie, M., & Edirisingha, P. (2007). Podcasting for learning. A*LISS Quarterly, 2*(4), 11-17.

Watson, J. (2010). A case study: Developing learning objects with an explicit learning design. *Electronic Journal of e-Learning, 8*(1), 41-50. Retrieved from http://www.ejel.org/volume8/issue1/p41

Watson, J. (2014). 'Sizing up' the online course: Adapting learning design to meet growing participant numbers. In S. Jager, L. Bradley, E. J. Meima, & S. Thouësny (Eds), *CALL Design: Principles and Practice; Proceedings of the 2014 EUROCALL Conference, Groningen, The Netherlands* (pp. 408-412). Dublin: Research publishing.net. doi:10.14705/rpnet.2014.000254

Watson, J., Dickens, A., & Gilchrist, G. (2008). The LOC tool: Creating a learning object authoring tool for teachers. *Proceedings of the World Conference on Educational Multimedia, Hypermedia and Telecommunications 2008, Association for the Advancement of Computing in Education, Vienna, Austria* (pp. 4626-4632). Retrieved from http://www.editlib.org/p/29030

Wiley, D. A. (2001). Connecting learning objects to instructional design theory: A definition, a metaphor, and a taxonomy. In D. Wiley (Ed.), *The instructional use of learning objects*. Agency for Instructional Technology. Retrieved from http://www.reusability.org/read/chapters/wiley.doc

10. Collaborative production of learning objects on French literary works using the LOC software

Christine Penman[1]

Abstract

This case study situates the collaborative design of learning objects (interactive online learning material) using the LOC (Learning Object Creator)[2] software in the context of language activities external to the core learning activities of language students at a UK university. It describes the creative and pedagogical processes leading to the creation of a series of learning objects on French literary works by and for students who do not formally study literature as part of their language degree. The study documents the initial set-up of projects and pragmatic constraints and affordances to team-based design. It reports on perception of this work by students and academic staff and reflects on the journey to building an open source library of discovery tools for a programme-based community of learners.

Keywords: authoring software, literature and language learning, collaborative design.

---

1. Edinburgh Napier University, Edinburgh, United Kingdom; C.Penman@napier.ac.uk.

2. http://loc.llas.ac.uk

How to cite this chapter: Penman, C. (2015). Collaborative production of learning objects on French literary works using the LOC software. In K. Borthwick, E. Corradini, & A. Dickens (Eds), *10 years of the LLAS elearning symposium: Case studies in good practice* (pp. 117-126). Dublin: Research-publishing.net. doi: 10.14705/10.14705/rpnet.2015.000272

Chapter 10

1. Context/rationale

Language degrees in Higher Education are often associated with the teaching and learning of literature. This is due to the potential of literature to carry cultural codes and to lend itself to critical and stylistic appraisal and debate, although the definition of the literary canon and the role that literature can play in second language acquisition are constantly under reappraisal (Carter, 2007). In the UK, literature on such courses is usually taught in English and tends to sit alongside language learning units. Conversely, university courses which do not offer literature as part of their language curriculum put forward applied practice which appeals in particular to the non-literary minded. This concerns more specifically joint honours degrees with, for example, business, law and tourism-related subject areas in their titles (e.g. BA Hons French with Marketing). However, among such cohorts of students there are also individuals who enjoy reading and while wanting to focus in the main on their communicative ability in the language, are interested in tapping into the wider discursive field that literature offers.

This case study relates the evolution of my thoughts as a university teacher on how contributions from literature could be made available to students for whom the study of literature is not a constituent part of their curriculum through the production of interactive learning materials (e-learning objects) using the LOC software. It touches upon the content of language teaching, on the place and contribution of technology in student learning and on issues of student motivation.

2. Aims and objectives

The aim of this case study is to present the processes behind the production and use in a blended mode of learning objects based on extracts from French literary works for university language students. It traces back various steps: what initiated my interest in the LOC tool from an academic perspective, the different phases of a subsidised project to involve students in the production of learning objects (subsequently referred to as LOs) and subsequent initiatives. It therefore charts the evolution of the locus of authorial control and discusses, in the process, pedagogical, technological and interactional issues throughout these different phases.

3. What I did

My first direct contact with the LOC software had occurred through response to a call for a training workshop which was facilitated by staff from LLAS[1] in 2010. Following my gradual involvement with the tool, I subsequently organised another workshop, in 2013, which widened access to colleagues from different academic fields throughout my university. The LOC can have applications well beyond the linguistic arena.

The LOC tool was developed by LLAS with the eLanguages[2] group at the University of Southampton to provide educators with user-friendly authoring software designed with a robust pedagogical approach based on a constructivist approach to learning. The tool can support a variety of media supports (text, images, sound, video, hyperlinks) and provides a scaffolded approach through non-graded (i.e. not formally assessed) activities with the learning objectives made clear to the learner as they progress through the learning object. The interactional activities occur through the provision of open and/or closed questions to which the learner responds through the approach selected by the LO creator (who can select from the following range: radio buttons, check boxes, drop down list, text entry box, gap fill, tick/cross column). Learners can check their answers against formative feedback which, depending on the type of questions asked, can be more or less comprehensive and open-ended. The possibilities afforded by learners through use of this tool are aptly captured by Hamilton-Hart (2010) who points to the usefulness of the feedback feature, especially when learners keep a record of their initial responses (since there is no

---

1. Centre for Languages, Linguistics and Area Studies (LLAS); www.llas.ac.uk

2. www.elanguages.ac.uk

Chapter 10

track recording facility on the tool) if they repeat the activities. This is facilitated by the fact that LOs are made available as standalone resources for students to access when they wish to.

The first learning objects I created were designed for formative feedback, to help language students revise aspects of grammar (e.g. on the formation of different levels of questions in French, which some students have issues with right up to the final year of their degree; on choice of tenses in the past (perfect vs. imperfect); on the use of complex pronouns). The LOs I initially created were based on a series of discrete questions rather than based on a primary document and were scheduled either in class or set in revision in directed learning activities.

3.1. First set of literary LOs: single authorship

The first LO based on a French literary extract which I created used two short extracts from a 19th century novel by Emile Zola, Au Bonheur des Dames. This is a novel set against the background of the creation of a department store in Paris, a commercial enterprise which heralded a revolution in consumer terms. The reason I selected this extract was because I had been struck by the modern appeal of the references to a range of marketing and advertising techniques which were very novel for the time but which still have resonance more than a century later. Since part of the material which we used in tutorials had a business angle, I felt that the extracts detailing the psychological manipulation of targeted female consumers (Extract 1) and the carefully planned positioning of goods in the store and various marketing and advertising strategies in place (Extract 2) had relevance for students studying in a business school and could stimulate reflection and discussions. In this instance one of the ancillary aims was to sensitise students to the contribution of literature to the recording of cultural processes. The activities which I designed were built upon the following sequence:

- a very short introduction to the work highlighting the focus on marketing techniques in the extracts i.e. bypassing in particular the romantic narrative and complexities of the novel;

- the textual extracts (under 250 words in both cases) with hyperlinks providing a translation into English of more complex words and phrases, followed by a recording of the extract;

- two staged activities: the first based on comprehension of the extracts, the second asking for interpretation of the techniques listed and personal evaluation in relation to modern time practices.

The feedback included the 'right' answer to binary questions or those based on a selection of possible answers and guiding formulations leaving space for personal appropriation of the content. All the metalanguage and questions were in French and pitched between levels B1 and B2 of the European Framework for languages. As the LOs are published as open source and accessible through a URL, these have been embedded in the institutional learning environment and set as directed learning to students on a number of occasions. The LOs have been well received and informal feedback from students on the learning activities has generally been positive, although some have found the 19th century language a barrier in spite of the linguistic scaffolding provided.

3.2. Second set of literary LOs: students and staff co-production in a funded project

Following reflection on ways to address a perceived need on some students' part for extension material and activities to expand cultural knowledge, and given the time constraints in lecturing slots, I successfully submitted a bid to an internal pedagogical fund to create more materials. The project proposed to compile a 'library' of culturally-oriented learning resources for language learners based on the active involvement of students and two academic staff. The process acknowledged the agency of learners in the compilation of relevant e-learning resources. Besides the benefit of an inclusive process (Ellis & Goodyear, 2009), at the end of the project the created resources were to be made available not only to the participants, to other French language learners at the university, but also to the wider community as open learning resources. Funding was granted for

Chapter 10

a research assistant[1] and for vouchers for student participants. The project was advertised to second year students working within Level B2 of the European Framework, later widened to further participants in fourth year and eventually involved six students. The initial plan was to work on a series of literary extracts from various authors and time periods to have a sample corpus on a timeline but after discussions with students and proposal of a range of texts, it was agreed to concentrate on one 19th-century text, Les Misérables by Victor Hugo. The work had resonance with the student group given the worldwide success of the English adaptation in the musical and film. This text also offers rich possibilities for linguistic and cultural explorations and provides a number of self-contained vignettes which can be extracted from the main text.

The students were briefed on the pedagogical remit of the learning objects and were invited to reflect and comment on existing resources prior to turning their hand to the creation of their own resource. They were subsequently allocated an extract from the 5 volumes of this lengthy and complex novel. The extracts were selected by the teaching assistant for their ability to encapsulate the historical background (such as Part 1 which provides a historical description, with a focus on prison population), to focus on the life and development of key characters (for instance Part 2 on Jean Valjean's childhood,) or on a pivotal moment in the narrative (such as Part 6 which relates the encounter between Cosette and Jean Valjean). All extracts provide opportunities for cultural readings. The students had to provide a series of linguistic and socio-cultural questions followed by feedback in a text-based format. They were invited to move from a detailed analysis to more open questions which would help situate the extract in a social, political and historical perspective and widen its relevance beyond the novel. The initial plan was to have group working sessions but as it proved difficult to find mutually suitable times, the students opted in the main for one-to-one interactions with the teaching assistant, initially in weekly personal contacts and later, once the teaching semester was over, by emails. This is reflected in the acknowledgements in the copyright section of the six resulting LOs which list one student and the project coordinators, apart from the first one which was the

---

1. I wish to take this opportunity to thank Dr Ana Zerón for all the work she did on this project.

product of more collaborative student work. The content produced by each student was negotiated with the assistant who subsequently carried out a substantial amount of editing. All students were offered the opportunity to transfer the text-based version to the LOC software but most declined it. Additional resources (such as pictures and audio sounds) and further editing were provided by myself as the project leader. The finished learning objects were disseminated among the student authors who provided positive informal feedback on their experience on creating this learning material. The LOs on Les Misérables were subsequently made available to the following cohort of second-year French language students.

3.3. Third set of literary LOs [in preparation]: dual authorship arising from student involvement in a reading group (supported by a blog)

The following year, the reflection which had provided the impetus to start building a 'library' of literature-based learning objects led me to organise a reading group for all interested students from Year 1 to 4. The book group was advertised on all French modules on the institutional Virtual Learning Environment (VLE) and twelve students volunteered, three of whom had previously worked on the LO project.

The students were offered a choice of two titles and opted for *Une année studieuse*, an autobiographical narrative published by Anne Wiazemsky in 2012, which revolves around the year 1967 when she met her husband-to-be, the film director Jean-Luc Godard. This book was selected for its cultural background of pre-May 1968 France, the central casting of a young woman close in age to the student group, and the potential for cultural comparisons over time and across cultural boundaries. References to prominent writers and artists of the time abound. I set up a blog for the reading group which met once a week over several weeks in the spring semester. The blog attracted contributions (in the form of questions and comments) from the students and a language assistant, and included vocabulary items and help to decipher some of the cultural references. The most protracted pieces of writing from students responded to a call for description of life in the 60s in their respective countries. The students reacted very positively to the book and to the reading group activities. To take this further a number of key passages which had stimulated lively discussions based on cultural interest have been identified by the language assistant[1] and myself for the creation of a new series of LOs. The extracts are based around central themes in the book: university teaching in 1967 and family relationships, both highlighting greater degrees of formality than modern day practices. The layout of the LOs is to follow the same pattern as that previously described, moving from close reading of the text to questions testing comprehension to an appreciation of the wider cultural implications and a reflection on their relation to contemporary issues. At the time of writing, around three learning objects are currently planned and once ready, these will be sent to the initial book group participants for comments and feedback before final editing.

4. Discussion

The LOs described above form part of a growing collection of literary capsules made available to learners of French through the institutional VLE. The resources are progressively published and made available as open resources for the wider community. Beyond the qualities of the scaffolded approach that the LOC design affords for the end users, there are a number of inherent benefits to having a series of activities available through a web link, related to availability, ease of reference and of embedding into learning environments.

The process, the preparation and production of these objects, has highlighted a number of recurring issues in terms of:

- selection of content: the challenge to identify literary extracts which, while offering scope for rich interpretations, can also be used as stand-alone units which do not require substantial embedding explanations;

---

1. I wish to thank Simona Camillini, our Leonardo language assistant, for the enthusiasm with which she took on this project.

- student participation: for collaborative production of material, the difficulty to identify times to meet, to sustain participation and ensure consistency in quality of content;

- staff involvement: the process requires substantial time investment, although productivity improves with practice.

The pedagogical funded projects brought to the fore a number of benefits as the development of material calls for creative, critical and analytical skills, and engages the students involved in a cumulative and constructive learning process. Those who have participated in that process have indicated that it was a positive and enjoyable learning experience in spite of demands on time. An indication of how students may perceive the relevance of this type of academic involvement in terms of transferable skills was provided by an email alert from Linkedin. Co-authorship on one of the LOs on Les Misérables was presented by one student on his site in the following terms: "mixing up the French language skills with the web development", which indicates that for that particular student both the content and technological sides of the product present valuable learning experiences and can be presented as such.

5. Conclusion

The creation of literary-based learning objects through a variety of approaches has been a creative response to the provision of additional resources for language students and to enable student involvement at different stages of the process. The e-learning objects compiled so far have been very well received by students interested in developing their linguistic and cultural knowledge through exposure to literary extracts. The format adopted in the third phase (i.e. the creation of two or three learning objects arising from discussions facilitated in a book group in a blended mode, subsequently tested and critiqued by the participants) seems to be a more sustainable way of continuing to develop material. Further development could be provided by researching more formally through interviews and focus groups students' responses to different types of material and scaffolded activities.

Chapter 10

References

Carter, R. (2007). Literature and language teaching 1986-2006: A review. *International Journal of Applied Linguistics, 17*(1), 3-13. doi:10.1111/j.1473-4192.2007.00130.x

Ellis, R., & Goodyear, P. (2009). *Students' experiences of e-learning in higher education: The ecology of sustainable innovation.* London: Routledge.

Hamilton-Hart, J. (2010). Using the LOC tool: An immersive learning experience for the user. *LLAS Liaison Magazine* (pp. 28-29). Retrieved from https://www.llas.ac.uk//resourcedownloads/179/liaison_july10.pdf

Links to LOCS

Au Bonheur des Dames
Partie 1 : http://loc.llas.ac.uk/lob/250/standalone/index.html
Partie 2 : http://loc.llas.ac.uk/lob/256/standalone/index.html

A la découverte de "Les Misérables"
Partie 1 : http://loc.llas.ac.uk/lob/1310/standalone/index.html
Partie 2 : http://loc.llas.ac.uk/lob/1316/standalone/index.html
Partie 3 : http://loc.llas.ac.uk/lob/1365/standalone/index.html
Partie 4 : http://loc.llas.ac.uk/lob/1372/standalone/index.html
Partie 5 : http://loc.llas.ac.uk/lob/1376/standalone/index.html
Partie 6 : http://loc.llas.ac.uk/lob/1377/standalone/index.html

11 Digital English – me, online, writing & academia

Ania Rolińska[1]

Abstract

This case study reports on the Digital English project, an experimental course in academic writing piloted with international students on a year-long pre-sessional programme. Inspired by Ulmer's (2003) *Mystory* project and Gauntlett's (2007) *Lego* research, the course concerns itself with the students' exploration of self at a sensitive time of transition across geographical, educational and cultural borders. To facilitate the journey, the project blended learning spaces (online and offline), literacies (home-based and academic) and modes (visual and verbal). As the culmination of their engagement with the themes such as digital literacy, visual culture and hypermedia, the learners created a visual artefact to tell their subjective self-story. This provided a stimulus for a more objective investigation conducted by peers. The analysis of the final multimodal displays showed that students tend to portray themselves as social beings, yet with individualistic goals in regard to their academic and professional success. In the project evaluation, the students described their learning experience as an enriching challenge, which tentatively shows that there is room for visuality, creativity and identity work in at least certain academic contexts.

Keywords: identity, visuality, creativity, digital literacy, academic development.

---

1. University of Glasgow, United Kingdom; annarolinska@yahoo.co.uk.

How to cite this chapter: Rolińska, A. (2015). Digital English – me, online, writing & academia. In K. Borthwick, E. Corradini, & A. Dickens (Eds), *10 years of the LLAS elearning symposium: Case studies in good practice* (pp. 127-137). Dublin: Research-publishing. net. doi:10.14705/rpnet.2015.000273

Chapter 11

1. Context/rationale

The *Digital English* project is an experimental writing course intending to facilitate the development of academic attributes such as creativity, critical thinking and reflection skills as presented in the *Matrix* devised by the University of Glasgow[1]. The course was trialled with international students preparing for a post-graduate study at a British university. The leading theme is self-exploration accompanied by examination of digital literacy, visual metaphors and crossovers between academic and home-oriented genres. The rationale for designing and offering such a course was twofold. Firstly, international students constitute almost one fifth of the total UK student body, with the Chinese student population having increased by 6% in 2012/13 (HESA, 2013). Apart from crossing the geographical borders, these students have to make a rapid transition in other domains too, including language and academic culture. The acceptable language competency level has been capped at 6.5 on the International English Language Testing System (IELTS) scale, which in terms of writing translates into an ability to write a range of texts of some complexity on various subjects, including abstract ones. This constitutes a challenging leap for many of the pre-sessional students who at the time of entry present 5-5.5 scores in writing and feel just comfortable enough to produce straightforward texts on familiar topics.

Settling into a new academic culture poses extra requirements in terms of skills and personal qualities such as independent and critical thinking. These refer to research and study *per se* but also, as transferable skills, to the application of creative, imaginative and innovative thinking to problem-solving processes. Some of the current approaches to writing might be suppressing creativity and innovation, and expository papers are likely to be interpreted by students as requests to regurgitate library knowledge. This can present a challenge for a learner with a language competency as described above, and complicated further by habits typical of their original academic culture. For example, Chinese students display a propensity to include narration or appeal to tradition in an effort to enliven their discourse. As a result, they may experience tension when

---

1. The University of Glasgow compiled a list of academic abilities, personal qualities and transferable skills which the students have the chance to acquire and develop during their studies http://www.gla.ac.uk/media/media_183776_en.pdf.

faced with British university writing conventions as they feel forced to give up on their original ideas. I am not advocating leniency in this respect but, through the project, suggest a different approach which embraces the students' needs, experiences and voices and so, hopefully, eases them into Western ways of thinking and writing.

The way in which the *Digital English* project respects the students' cultural histories and complex subject positions is through asking them to reflect on those subjectivities. This is achieved by harnessing visuality, digital hypermedia and multimodality, a second leitmotif of the project. *Digital English* draws on Gauntlett's (2007) *Lego* research and Ulmer's (2003) *Mystory* project. The former concerns itself with an exploration of identity through play with building blocks and discovers that certain subjectivities are more easily expressed using the visual-spatial logic than through language. The latter exploits the internet as a medium that "puts us in a new relation to writing" (Ulmer, 2003, p. 2), both as writers and readers. This means the traditional notion of literacy does not suffice and has to be expanded to include new strategies such as linkage, collage, juxtaposition and image reasoning. Imagistic and hypertextual writing orients the student toward interrelations, overlaps and recursive patterns, which introduces creativity into learning (Csikszentmihalyi, 1993; Ulmer, 2003). This is possible because visual syntax follows a different logic aligned with relationality and synchronicity. This way it allows unexpected conceptual links to be forged while a conventionally structured text imposes processing information in a linear, sequential fashion, which may prevent the unexpected from surfacing. Engagement with digital hypermedia as well as the associative and lateral logic of creative thinking might help students become active, responsible and critical consumers and producers of information and knowledge.

2. Aims and objectives

The experimental course focuses on issues of digital literacy, with the particular attention to the visual turn, and attempts to harness the learner's creativity by asking them to produce their own self-story, following the premise that the unexamined life is not worth living. This digital artefact was then embedded into a collectively written report. While the former allowed the student to experiment with visual metaphors to express highly subjective notions, the latter was more academically oriented and required the students to take on a role of a detached researcher. Interweaving home- and university-based genres and discourses intended to assist the student in making a transition between cultures as well as language competencies characteristic for each of the contexts and discussed in the previous section. Adding an interpretative layer of an academic commentary also attempted to explore the value of creativity and visuality for academic development. Achieving the main goal was aligned with a number of process-oriented aims, such as:

- facilitating reflection on identity and subjectivity in order to gain a better understanding of one's self in the context of academic study and the related cross-linguistic and -cultural transitions;

- raising a general awareness of digital literacy with a particular focus on visual metaphors, linkage, multimodality as well as privacy, online persona and copyright;

- developing evaluation and reflection skills through assessing the implications of self-awareness and digital literacy for learning, particularly in a higher education context;

- developing practical skills in the use of digital tools, e.g. photo editors, web search engines, Creative Commons licences, Google Docs, wikis, hyperlinks, blogs, and zooming presentation software.

3. What I did

The course was delivered in a blended mode at the University of Glasgow Language Centre to a group of 14 international students preparing for a postgraduate study. The group consisted of Chinese and Middle-Eastern students with IELTS scores of 5.5-6 in writing. We met twice a week in a computer lab over the period of 10 weeks. During the 1.5-hour sessions the students were introduced to the main concepts of the course through reading/listening tasks, followed by individual and collaborative research and writing activities as well as guided group discussions.

Figure 1. Digital English wiki homepage

During the face-to-face sessions, they were also introduced to the main web tools and provided with numerous practice opportunities so that they felt sufficiently comfortable to use them unassisted at home. The main hub was a wiki[1] (Figure 1) which outlined all the activities and provided links to core and further resources. Each student set up a Gmail account to use for the project purposes. This was dictated by convenience as Gmail can easily be linked to Blogger and Google Docs, the other two tools extensively used throughout the course. The blogs were used for reflection and submission of individual tasks. Their content was fed to the wiki via RSS to aggregate all the student work and make it easier to read and comment on postings. The Google Docs were used for

---

1. The wiki can be accessed here: http://digitalenglish-mystory.wikispaces.com/

collaboration, for example to work on documents in groups either as authors or commentators.

The course was organised into four sections, reflecting Csikszentmihalyi's (1993) idea of a 5-stage 'creativity flow' process. Each stage included a sequence of in-class and homework tasks that directly or indirectly linked to the main project outcomes (the time frames given in brackets refer to initially planned timings).

3.1. Preparation (week 1)

In this climate-setting week the students approached the main theme of self through listening to an artist's informal reflection and an academic lecture on identity. They set up a Google account, which allowed them to start a blog. They were introduced to photo search engines and Creative Commons in order to locate visual metaphors representing their actual/imagined/desired subjectivity, which assisted them in the preliminary reflection on their identity. The next step entailed linking the reflection with an exploration of graduate attributes. This helped them establish personal goals for the duration of the course.

3.2. Incubation (weeks 2-4)

In this exploratory phase the students worked more closely with the course main themes of identity, creativity and visual culture as well as techniques of hypertext and image collages. They collaborated on transforming a quasi-biographical text into a hypertext, an exercise in annotation, linkage and content visualisation. Constructing the hypertext required greater engagement with the themes and a more in-depth analysis. Additionally, they benefitted from working in groups as well as having to think critically by providing constructive feedback via comments on the other group's hypertext. Subsequently, through working with Gauntlett's (2007) ideas stemming from the *Lego* research, the students examined the issues of visuality and their potential usefulness in connecting ideas and creating new understandings of their selves. As a personalised follow-up, each learner created their own identity visualisation in the form of either an interactive image collage (using Thinglink) or a Prezi presentation, with written captions or a voiceover respectively. The artefact created this way constituted a multimodal record of the students' inner voice elaborating on their subjective understanding of their professional, cultural, familial and academic circumstances.

3.3. Elaboration and evaluation (weeks 5-9)

The students were divided into small groups and allocated 2-3 digital artefacts constructed by their classmates. Their task was to develop a more objective and stylistically more formal analysis to problematise the student's everyday experience based on the background research. The final story-within-story was expected to be a hypertext, using hyperlinks, visuals and texts and so becoming an amalgam of not only the student's subjectivities but also modes and styles. However, this task proved ambitious and in the end, the students produced a written report analysing and interpreting their peers' visuals with references to existing research such as Gauntlett's (2007) *Lego* study mentioned earlier. The end result was a multimodal display blending the private and the academic in terms of content, genres, styles and modes.

3.4. Reflection (week 10)

The students presented the displays to a wider student body as well as a group of tutors during a mingling event. They also reflected on their engagement in the creative process throughout the course by filling in a questionnaire and completing a final reflective blog post.

4. Discussion

The design of *Digital English* aspires to have roots in a blend of cognitivism and critical pedagogy. The in-depth and creative exploration of own subjectivity, which consistently requires the students to map out the links between the familiar and the unfamiliar by embedding the visual artefact in an academic enquiry, is in line with cognitivism principles (Shor, 1993). So is the inclusion of

Chapter 11

regular reflective blog entries – the students were asked, for example, to reflect on academic attributes such as creativity, dedication to innovation and criticality or on the role of visual culture in academia. The reflections often aimed to engage the students in a metadata analysis, leading them to become more self-aware and -directed learners. As a tutor, I tried to act as a question- and problem-poser as well as a provider of formative feedback to facilitate the self-regulation processes.

Apart from strengthening thinking skills, the course initiated the development of critical consciousness in the students so that they become more self-organised, self-educated and critically literate. This goal could largely be achieved by undertaking the task of presenting a visual testimony of oneself and having it elaborated on by peers through references to academic sources. Through this inquiry into their selves I hoped the students would recognise and possibly challenge myths, values and language that may be underlying their behaviours and actions through dialogues in class or on the blogs. The main findings from the analyses performed by the student researchers showed that the students tend to portray themselves as social beings, entangled in networks and shaped by relationships, in line with Gauntlett's (2007) research. Simultaneously, there is a degree of self-determination represented by frequent references to setting and achieving personal goals. Interestingly, the students did not evade articulating less positive points in their identity construction and so they often alluded to their doubts and concerns regarding their personal life and academic development. The analysis also revealed and so drew attention to the cultural differences in values. For instance, it was interesting to see how the students discovered and made sense of diverse perceptions of family patterns or gender roles existing in their peers' cultures, which potentially made a useful contribution to developing a cross-cultural awareness among the students, a crucial competency in the globalised academia.

Throughout the course, the students actively engaged in the process of learning, also in a sense of having a direct influence on the ongoing activities. The learning spaces, both online and offline, were organised in such a way that they aimed to be:

- participatory – students initiated and maintained dialogic blogs;

- situated – contextualisation prominently featured in the course activities;

- critical – self and social reflection was prioritised;

- democratic – the students were engaged in indirect evaluation of the course syllabus through their blog reflections and in-class discussions; materials and activities were often adapted 'on the go' as an immediate response to the students' needs and interests; questioning was encouraged and opposing opinions were dealt with sensitively; for instance, when an engineering student doubted merits of analysing art-oriented reflections for academic development we discussed opportunities for transferral of such knowledge and skills;

- dialogic – the students were asked to recast their experience in their own words and through images;

- desocialised from passivity – the instructions were often deliberately left open, the models were provided only occasionally and it was constantly stressed that independence and creativity are favoured over simple replication;

- research-oriented – the research was undertaken by both the students and the tutor, the latter for example with a view of providing appropriate and informed feedback.

All these elements are highly reminiscent of the socially critical approach (Shor, 1993).

As regards the evaluation of the pedagogical usefulness of the project, interviews with students as well as the final feedback survey showed that overall the course succeeded in meeting the learning outcomes and stimulating the students' self-awareness. Each of the participants might have developed it to a different degree and in different direction, being it in a personal or more academic sphere of their life. They particularly welcomed the development of digital literacy, a positive finding as a brief questionnaire on technology use at the beginning of the course showed a varied use of social web tools among this particular cohort. In their feedback, the students commented on their heightened sense of ownership and responsibility for their online space and expressed appreciation of being able to connect to and have a dialogue with peers and experts. At the same time, some of them voiced concerns over privacy and data protection as well as the netiquette of commenting on others' work. They noticed benefits of the web for academic and social development, including greater opportunities for social inclusion and integration into the Western society. In terms of more personalised academic gains, one would-be social science student appreciated familiarisation with visual methodologies to conduct richer and more in-depth analyses of research subjects. Generally, the students were able to see the applicability of the skills developed during the project in the further study. As one of them put it, the project showed them how to think 'out of the box', which demonstrated a growing awareness of critical thinking, acknowledging multiple perspectives and nurturing curiosity and open mind when researching a given topic.

5. Conclusion

Overall, the students considered participation in the *Digital English* project a useful and enjoyable exercise – 'a happy learning process' to use a quote from one of them – worth recommending to their peers. It was a useful experience for me, too. Initially I had been concerned that there might be little appreciation of more creativity- and visuality-oriented teaching approaches to development of academic skills and attributes. I was very tentative in introducing the idea to the students but their response convinced me that the project is worth pursuing and developing further. I hope that sharing the idea through this case study opens up a discussion about the place and value of visuality, creativity and identity work in academia, in at least some contexts, as well as provides the teaching community with ideas of possible multimodal pedagogical activities.

References

Csikszentmihalyi, M. (1993). *Creativity: Flow and the psychology of discovery and invention.* New York: HarperCollins Publishers.

Gauntlett, D. (2007). *Creative explorations: New approaches to identities and audiences.* London: Routledge.

HESA. (2013). Statistical first release 197 – Non-UK domicile students. *Higher Education Statistics Agency.* Retrieved from https://www.hesa.ac.uk/stats

Shor, I. (1993). Education is politics: Paulo Freire's critical pedagogy. In P. McLaren & P. Leonard (Eds), *Paulo Freire: A critical encounter* (pp. 25-35). London: Routledge. doi:10.4324/9780203420263

Ulmer, G. L. (2003). *Internet invention: From literacy to electracy.* New York: Pearson Education.

12 The grammar movie project

Edith Kreutner[1]

Abstract

In this case study, I will show how directing a movie on grammar can help students improve their oral skills as well as their language competency, team working and planning skills, and also teach them about learning itself. I will present an innovative teaching project that uses the medium of film to get students engaged with grammar and that aims at providing them with a form of assessment that makes revision by the students possible and gives control of the final version to the student.

Keywords: movie, language awareness, teamwork, collaboration, creativity, grammar, revision, exam preparation.

1. Context/rationale

Following the urge to modernise assessment methods for a second year German language degree course at the University of Bristol, the language team of the German Department in the School of Modern Languages developed a new method for oral exams. The tutor-led oral exam for students of German has been replaced with a group-based project, the grammar movie project. Previously, the German oral exam had consisted of a 10 minute talk/discussion about newspaper or magazine articles and took place on an individual basis in the tutors' offices. The mark was thus a result of a one-off, 10 minute performance without the opportunity for the student to revise, go over his/her performance and with little

---

1. University of Bristol, United Kingdom; edith.kreutner@bristol.ac.uk.

How to cite this chapter: Kreutner, E. (2015). The grammar movie project. In K. Borthwick, E. Corradini, & A. Dickens (Eds), *10 years of the LLAS elearning symposium: Case studies in good practice* (pp. 139-149). Dublin: Research-publishing.net. doi:10.14705/rpnet.2015.000274

chance to prepare properly as mock-exams with the teacher would be too time and labour intensive.

2. Aims and objectives

The aim of our oral exam revamp was to come up with a form of assessment that:

- incorporates outcomes of modern research into pedagogy and learning;

- allows for the use of new media;

- gives the students an opportunity to rehearse, practise and use feedback from peers to improve their oral production before handing in the final work for marking;

- combines several aspects of the curriculum;

- takes the student from solitary confinement to a helpful team working environment;

- invites the students to reflect on their own learning;

- boosts student enthusiasm through the use of new media and the creative freedom of the project;

- increases employability: organisation and teamwork skills are a highly sought after assets on the job market and many previous students mentioned that listing the project on their CVs has resulted in very positive feedback from employers.

With this project, we combined the oral exam with other fields from the curriculum and decided to address grammar needs directly. There is significant dispute amongst scholars whether grammar should be taught explicitly or whether grammar awareness comes with exposure to language. Research into the subject provides evidence for both sides of the argument (Ellis, 2006; Norris & Ortega, 2000). Irrespective of which side one is on, everyday life proves that teachers are faced with the conundrum that instructed knowledge can often be reproduced and rattled off by students but is not incorporated into active language production.

3. What I did

Once our students reach the second year of their German degree, they should all have a substantial knowledge of German grammar, but reality is different and leaves the teacher in a dilemma: how do we make sure that the teaching caters for everyone's needs? These are the needs of the grammar geek who knows even the smallest detail and also the needs of students who find it very hard, struggle and tend to blank out grammar altogether. This dilemma is largely due to the different approaches to grammar teaching the students have been exposed to in the wide variety of schools that they have come from before they all join the same language course at university level. The grammar movie project was started in 2010 to tackle this with an innovative student-friendly teaching approach that utilises new media, respects different learning styles and learning backgrounds and sets an example as a multi-dimensional approach to grammar learning.

After a short exercise-based repetition of the most important grammar topics in the first teaching block, the students are split into groups of two to three and have to select one of those already familiar grammar topics, but are advised to choose –under the guidance of their tutor– the one they feel is their weakest point. Exercising their own creativity, the students are asked (outside class hours) to produce a 5-8 minute educative and instructive video in the target language that is meant to explain the characteristics and important features of their chosen grammar topic. This movie is then part of a 15-20 minute grammar teaching session, which is fully managed and led by the students, who also have to support their session with exercises they see fit to strengthen further what they have just taught. Putting together a concise hand-out explaining the grammar topic in a way that helped them themselves to understand their topic is also part of the assignment. In order to help students who find keeping to a strict schedule hard or who might have worked away on the wrong tangent, all teams have to meet with the teacher a week before they are due to present. At that point, they have to present their plans and submit their hand-outs. By doing this, the teacher can make sure that hand-outs are fit to be given to the rest of the class and that the team is on track.

The presentation itself includes a short introduction to the grammar topic, the showing of the grammar movie and several exercises. All of this is to be done by the students; they become teachers for the period of the presentation and also for a short while again when grammar specific homework, which is always given to the class at the end of each grammar movie presentation, is corrected at the beginning of the next class. A substantial reflective journal about their experiences, learning processes and outcomes has to be handed in to the lecturer at the end. Each year, tutors then select suitable videos to be incorporated in their year 1 grammar teaching, often as part of our online grammar course. In order to make sure that all teachers on the course are aware of the research background, the underlying teaching methodology, the guidelines, and specific staff training are offered. Furthermore, members of staff are encouraged to participate in conferences and seminars suitable to the field.

3.1. Guidelines and marking criteria

Clear guidelines are mandatory for the success of the project. Student feedback from previous years, results of meetings with fellow lecturers teaching the unit, and questions and advice from scholars met at conferences and international seminars where the grammar movie project was presented (such as the 8th LLAS e-learning symposium) are all incorporated and we are still improving the project. Whereas students were given oral instructions in the first year of the project, they are now supplied with a multi-page handbook with all the guidelines, clear instructions, tips where to get help and support (other than the teacher), rental equipment for the filming, helpful links and ideas for further reading. The handbook also contains a breakdown of the weighing of the grammar movie project within the framework of the course and of the project itself. It is crucial for the success of the project that the students are informed about the weighing of the sets of criteria and that they know about the marking criteria in the first place. Experience from previous years has shown that some students get carried away with the artistic side of the project and are oblivious to the fact that even though the artistic aspect does count –albeit for only 10%–, the grammar movie project is not a unit in Film Studies but first and foremost a German language assessment. Explaining the reasoning behind the aims and objectives of the project to the students, talking them through it and highlighting the 'whys' and 'hows' improves the student experience and means that they, at the same time, get another chance to learn about their own learning.

The grammar movie project is predominantly a group project, and aspects of group collaboration, collaborative thinking about the best way to achieve the criteria and reaching the common goal as well as tackling obstacles on this way together (such as pronunciation, vocabulary, intonation, spelling and grammatical accuracy but also technical aspects such as cutting, sound, putting the handout together, time management and the creative site as a whole) are central to the project. Thus, the mark awarded goes out to the group as a whole. This also encourages students to help each other perform better. Only the final reflective report is marked for the individual student.

The main focus of attention is on oral performance. The students are urged to speak during the movie; there must not be silent characters or students that only fulfil the role of director or camera man. Instructions in the grammar movie guidelines and also verbal instructions during class are making it very clear that the students are in charge; they decide which version of their movie they present. Thus, they are given the opportunity to revise and rework their project as many times as they want until they then agree on a final version on which the mark is going to be based. The previous version of their oral exam did not offer this opportunity to revise, to fine-tune aspects of pronunciation or intonation by recording sections again or to eliminate mistakes altogether by using the knowledge pool of the entire group. Different levels of language skills and awareness within the groups will lead to the opportunity for correction amongst peers without the inclusion of a teacher. The use of digital video recording equipment allows multiple recordings of which the students can then choose the one they are most happy with. This selection process is again a process of critical reflection, of dealing with language in an analytical way, selecting their best version.

3.2. Feedback and feed-forward

After their presentation, the students are invited to an extensive feedback session, both as a group and as individuals. The tutor incorporates material from the reflective reports into the session, thus encouraging the students once again to reflect on their own learning experience and performance. Besides talking about the overall presentation, they are also given written feedback on their oral performance and feed-forward.

4. Discussion

In 2013, the project was evaluated with a comprehensive questionnaire, the results of which have lead to improvements of the project and the handbook. In the following, I will present the results of this questionnaire as well as excerpts of the reflective reports and answers to the open questions. Figure 1 and Figure 2 illustrating the results are given below. Due to the small numbers of students each year, the number of completed questionnaire is low at 29, but nonetheless representative of the cohort as most students returned the questionnaire.

The evidence of the questionnaire backed up by observation during the project itself shows clearly that the students reflect on their own language skills and also shows willingness to improve them. 80%, for example, selected their grammar topic on the basis of what they found hard or usually struggled with.

Figure 1. Effects of the grammar movie project

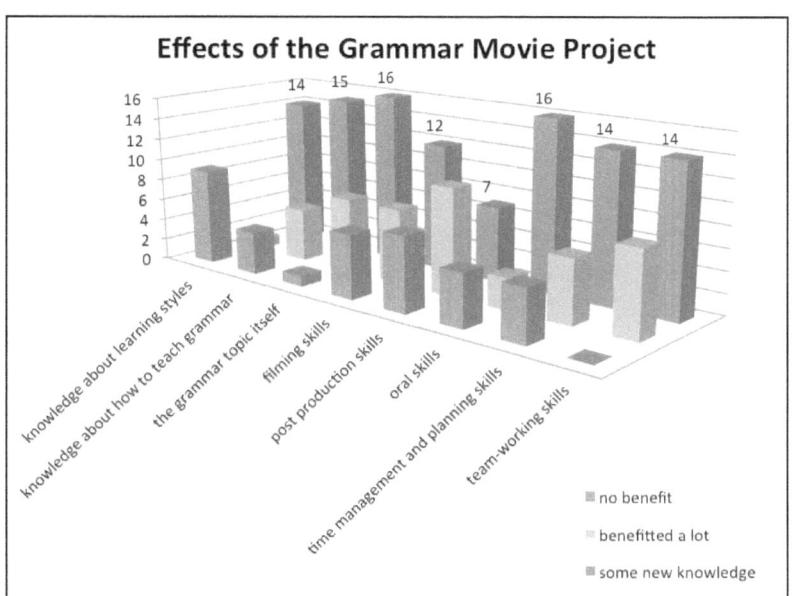

Figure 2. Self-assessment of grammar knowledge prior and post grammar movie project; the students had to rate their knowledge, 1 being the lowest score, 10 the score reflecting the highest level of knowledge

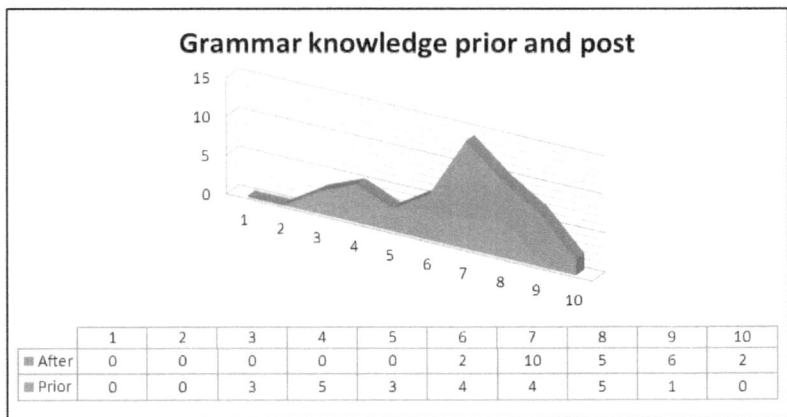

Thorough understanding of the subject is a prerequisite for teaching and encourages students to dig deep into grammar: it is intrinsic motivation to know more. When asked to estimate their knowledge about their specific grammar topic prior and post project, a significant increase can be seen in the data set (see Figure 1 and Figure 2).

By being put in the teaching role, the students have to talk about and apply logical connections, grammatical classifications and useful terms, and are no longer mere sponges but are encouraged to engage critically with the material.

The results also highlight that the students could gain team-working skills as well as other important skills such as time management. Because the project involves various stages, and through its nature requires good structuring (as not only the filming but also the cutting and editing take up a lot of time), many students mentioned that they would take away valuable lessons.

The students themselves are in charge of their final version: they are actively encouraged to re-record passages they are not happy with, to discuss how their project can be improved and to only hand in/present what they consider to be their best piece. 88% used the opportunity to re-record passages to improve their performance. This aspect was also mentioned numerous times in the reflective reports:

> "As we filmed, we noticed errors and room for improvement and honed the performance" (A.E., 2013).

> "We completed each part of our project in good time ensuring we had enough time to overview and edit any work that we produced. This gave us a good opportunity to analyse our oral performance and encouraged us to listen carefully for our own and others' grammar mistakes. The filming process was also useful to improve listening skills and to help focus on accuracy in speaking, particularly word order that I am aware can be a frequent source of errors in my spoken language" (A.B., 2013).

"The language skills that we practiced will undoubtedly be useful in future study, not only the grammar we learnt but also the ability to speak clearly and more fluently" (A.S., 2013).

That the project also led to an improvement in their oral skills is underlined by the students' self-assessment: 67% were of the opinion that their oral skills had improved because of the project.

The results of the students' self-evaluation show that through completing the grammar movie project, the students not only enhanced their grammar knowledge and language awareness but also their agility in using the language. There was a clear increase in their self-assessed level of grammar knowledge. That this is not just theoretical knowledge but rather language awareness was emphasised by the students numerous times in their written reports.

"The filming process was also useful to improve listening skills and to help focus on accuracy in speaking, particularly word order that I am aware can be a frequent source of errors in my spoken language. As a result I feel our presentation was much more grammatically accurate due to an increased awareness of the errors we regularly make" (A.B., 2013).

"I feel that by writing a script we came across vocabulary and grammar structures that we weren't certain of so we really had to take time to work it out, thus we practiced grammar we found difficult and learnt new vocabulary" (A.S., 2013).

"Having to explain a topic to others really requires you to fully understand the grammar yourself in the first place, and this exercise highlighted where I needed to brush up on my grammar myself!" (I.A., 2013).

"I had to learn anything I didn't fully understand in order to put it into my own words and explain it" (E.S., 2013).

"We were able to collect as much information as possible through research and revision (online, in grammar books and previous class notes and work) then continually revisit and edit our tutorial to make it accurate, comprehensive and with as few mistakes as possible" (I.A., 2013).

"From my own topic I've learnt that I understand and retain grammar rules much more efficiently by contextualising them in realistic situations or dialogue, and will be sure to do this when I come to revise for the summer exams" (F.P., 2014).

5. Conclusion

A major question in language methodology is 'does it help to know the rule in order to use grammar correctly?' (Schulz, 2002[1]). The results of teaching with the grammar movie project in place as an assessment method that combines grammar revision with an oral assessment clearly show that "reflecting on language use and using language do not have to be opposites" (Hutz, 2006, p. 22).

The results prove this: selective grammar teaching can lead to building language awareness, if it is carried out according to the age and learning level of the learner and provides ample opportunity and space for exploration and trial and error. The grammar movie project agrees with the current trend of incorporating a discussion of grammatical structures in the communicative context thereby encouraging the learner to become aware of the relation between meaning and form. But the benefits of the project do not stop here: working on this multi-faceted project, the students acquire additional transferable skills, such as team-working, problem-management, time-management and software-skills. The results of the questionnaire so far are proof for the success of the project in various aspects of the university curriculum.

---

1. Article title originally in German.

References

Ellis, R. (2006). Current issues in the teaching of grammar: An SLA perspective. *TESOL Quarterly, 40*(1), 83-107. doi:10.2307/40264512

Hutz, M. (2006). "Lemonade for Sale!" Grammatik im aufgabeorientierten Unterricht. *Der Fremdsprachliche Unterricht Englisch, 84*, 22-25.

Norris, J. M., & Ortega, L. (2000). Effectiveness of L2 instruction: A research synthesis and quantitative meta-analysis. *Language Learning, 50*(3), 417-528. doi:10.1111/0023-8333.00136

Schulz, R. A. (2002). Hilft es die Regel zu wissen um sie anzuwenden? Das Verhältnis von metalinguistischem Bewusstsein und grammatischer Kompetenz in DaF. *Die Unterrichtspraxis/Teaching German, 35*(1), 15-24. doi:10.2307/3531951

13. Tapping technology in creating product development studies: Reflections on an ESP-business project

Aiden Yeh[1]

Abstract

This paper describes a teacher's reflections on a technology-enhanced project-based learning approach to teaching an ESP-business lesson on product development, which is part of the curriculum for Conference English and Meetings Practice (CEMP), a business-track course for the Adult Continuing Education program at a private university in southern Taiwan. The project aimed to provide students with the opportunity to simulate the process of creating an improved product concept based on target market needs and produce a marketing campaign. Students worked on blending traditional materials with technology throughout the learning process from brainstorming, sketching, and presenting visually creative layouts. One of the caveats of undertaking this project was the time involved in production. Similar to real-life marketing scenarios, the crucial element was shooting and editing the videos and the making of the product prototype. Nonetheless, they were able to overcome those challenges and their product studies showed their flair for creativity and ingenuity.

Keywords: ESP-business English, product-development studies, project-based learning, blended learning, mobile technology.

---

1. Wenzao Ursuline University of Languages, Taiwan; aidenyeh@yahoo.com.

How to cite this chapter: Yeh, A. (2015). Tapping technology in creating product development studies: Reflections on an ESP-business project. In K. Borthwick, E. Corradini, & A. Dickens (Eds), *10 years of the LLAS elearning symposium: Case studies in good practice* (pp. 151-161). Dublin: Research-publishing.net. doi:10.14705/rpnet.2015.000275

Chapter 13

1. Context/rationale

Conference English and Meetings Practice (CEMP/會議英文與演練) is a required three-credit course in the business-track program for English-major students enrolled in the Division of Continuing Education of a private university in southern Taiwan. This course aims to enhance students' English communication skills within a business setting. The main goal is to enhance proficiency in all four skills (listening, speaking, reading, and writing) so they can effectively use the language in various business contexts.

The course content covers a wide range of corporate concepts such as mergers and acquisitions, and they also need to improve their career skills that are essential in performing their work duties. Giving presentations, engaging in project-based tasks, writing business reports or proposals are examples of transferable skills that students learn from this course. Language activities, i.e. grammar structures and vocabulary exercises, are based on authentic materials such as articles from leading business magazines and newspapers. Web-based technology, mobile devices, and digital technologies are blended into a traditional learning environment. Students learn how to access digital learning materials from the course's e-learning platform provided by the university; they also make use of their smartphones to do online searches, take pictures of lecture slides projected via an overhead projector, and share notes and ideas via mobile chat applications such as Line, WhatsApp, Facebook, etc.

In addition to teaching content knowledge, teaching CEMP also requires good coaching skills, thus encouraging and motivating students to take part in active learning is important in setting up a learning environment where fun and creativity are supported. This is why technology-enhanced project-based activities are an effective pedagogical strategy for delivering hands-on learning; they can enhance students' understanding of the key concepts being taught. Students do not simply regurgitate memorised information, but they engage themselves in creating something that would provide evidence of learning.

2. Aims and objectives

The product development project described here was given as the final task for the units on innovation (product improvement) and marketing communications (creating print and TV commercials). The aim of the activity was to provide students with the opportunity to simulate the process of creating a product concept based on target market needs, and to produce a marketing campaign for the product. The current advances in digital technology and its applications in product design and advertising have contributed greatly to its use in the classroom to simulate creative design techniques which provide students with the opportunity to enhance their technical skills. Thus, it was imperative that students had an awareness of existing mobile and digital technologies which they can integrate into their project plan and ensure effective application which is aligned with their learning needs and outcomes. This pedagogical approach also allows students to work on blending traditional materials with accessible technology throughout the learning process from brainstorming and sketching to presentation of prototype studies and creative video campaigns.

3. What I did

The use of technology in the project complements the traditional approaches to delivering and managing a planned learning process. The project required careful planning and time management. It took about four to five weeks (one class meeting = three hours per week) to complete.

First, I explained to the class the aims and outcomes of this project, how they are going to do it, and the reasons for doing it, emphasising how their learning is going to benefit them. For the first two hours, I covered the basic concepts of product improvement, practiced oral conversations, read articles and went through a list of vocabulary and grammar structures that they could use when presenting their product proposals. I also made sure that all digital lecture materials and exercise sheets were uploaded to the e-learning platform for their perusal. To provide extra learning guidance to help students learn and retain the new knowledge and information, I gave sufficient examples of product improvements and their ad campaigns by showing them digital print and video ads.

For the third hour, I discussed with them the details of the project. I went through the task requirements and gave instructions on how to proceed. I asked them to form small groups (N= 42; four to six students per group) so they could begin their initial brainstorming of a product idea and a tentative product name (see "3.1. Brainstorming" below). I gave students the freedom to choose their own group members. Some had difficulty joining other groups due to various reasons, from being unfamiliar with other classmates to being stubborn and unwilling to work with others. I had to remind them that learning to work in teams is a professional skill that they can use in real business situations. Thankfully, all groupings were sorted out in the end.

3.1. Brainstorming

During the first group brainstorming session, I asked students to think of and discuss a product that needs improvement or a consumer need that is not being met by any product. I asked them to search online using their mobile devices to help them with their discussion. They had to be able to show and tell me which aspect of the product required changing. They needed to show their innovation by sketching, either using a smartphone app or on paper, to see what improvements they had come up with. As I walked around, I listened in to group discussions, offered suggestions when needed, and provided support and constructive feedback. Providing constructive feedback is crucial in building their confidence; and once that confidence is established, they can carry it with them throughout the semester and beyond.

I asked them to upload a photo of their drawings to Padlet, an online wall poster I created for this activity. Links and guidelines were given to help them complete the task. The Padlet page was later projected on the screen, so everybody saw what sorts of ideas were collaboratively developed during that time (Figure 1).

Figure 1. Padlet wall[1]

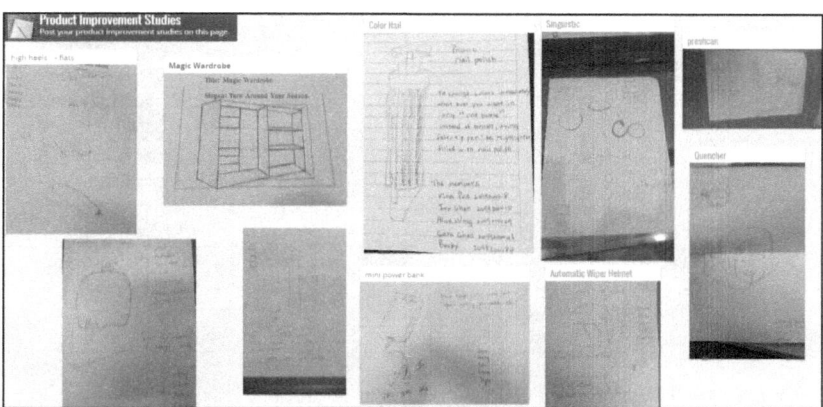

Table 1 below shows the product improvement studies, which exhibit the kinds of products each group had chosen, the improvements on product features, brand studies, and campaign slogans. All ideas were unique and had a potential market niche. For example, the S-shaped bluetooth-enabled translator device 'Singuistic' (an amalgamation of the letter "S" and "inguistic" from the word "Linguistics"), has the ability to simultaneously translate what other people are saying to your set or preferred language, seems like a product of the future.

Another example is PresshCan which is a trash bin which automatically presses the trash to save space and therefore saves money on garbage bags. Refer to Table 1 for more product descriptions.

Table 1. Product improvement studies

Group	Product	Product Improvement	Brand	Slogan
1	Trash Can	Trash can with an automatic function that presses trash, giving more space for more trash	PresshCan	• Stop being busy with trash • Save space • Save time

---

1. http://padlet.com/aidenyeh/w9mgwr0kqyqw

Chapter 13

2	Bluetooth-enabled Translator	S-shaped Bluetooth device that gives users instant simultaneous translation to different languages.	Singuistic	• The gateway to the world • Hear the word • Hear the world
3	Bodywash	Eight different fragrances in one bottle	Rico Bodywash	• Enrich your life • Wonderful with Rico! Eight-in-one
4	Helmet with wiper	Helmet with built-in wiper; wipes away rain or wet substance to give the user a better view of the road	RainyStar Automatic Wiper Helmet	• Amazing automatic wiper helmet • Wipe on! • Make it clear!
5	Rotating wardrobe	Allows users to store seasonal clothing; hide clothes that are not needed; rotating wardrobe	Magic Wardrobe	• Magic wardrobe • Turn around your season
6	Double-purpose shoes	High-heel shoes; heels can be tucked away under the soles	FIT shoes	• Free your feet, wear FIT
7	Helmet with water tube	Allows users to drink water (or any content) using the built-in tube on the helmet	Quencher	• Quench your thirst
8	Multi-purpose USB	USB that charges the device, serves as digital file storage also	Mini-Helper	• Amazing Mini! • Recharge! • Storage! • Advantage!
9	Nail Polish	8 different nail polish colours in a pen; can be applied instantly; super quick dry polish	Nail It!	• Just nail it right away!

3.2. Scaffolding skills

For the second class meeting, a lecture and workshop on creative writing (i.e. ad copies and slogans) and technical skills review (video editing skills) were given. Using PowerPoint (PPT) slides, we looked at famous slogans of different corporations, what made them tick and what kinds of ads flopped. In producing their video, I gave examples of free video programs (Windows Movie Maker, Power Director, etc.) which our university provides and they can access on all the computers in the library and computer laboratories. Some students already had existing skills in using video editing tools, but to be sure that everyone had the necessary skills, I spent time showing them again how to easily create a video using PPT slides and Windows Movie Maker (WMM). At this stage, they had to finalise their slogans and ad copies, and product prototype for those who already finished with their copies. They should also have clearly outlined each team member's roles and responsibilities for production week (third week).

3.3. Product prototypes

By the third week, they worked on making a prototype for their product and started shooting their commercials[1]. From the digital footage they chose images that they could use for the print ad. In this way, there was consistency in the overall approach and look of their product campaign. Some groups shot a few scenes either in the classroom[2] (staging a set) or on campus. However, all these were done outside class hours and in their own spare time. In some cases, groups had to go on location shooting. This happened when the shots or images they needed could not be produced on the school grounds.

Below is a screenshot of some of the product studies. From paper sketches to the actual prototypes, the studies show students' talents and ingenuity. Some products were difficult to create, so they used alternative ways to show the product improvements.

One strategy they used was to manipulate a photo image using photo editor and tweaked it to reveal improved product features (see Figure 2). For FIT Shoes, the group thought of using almost identical shoes in their commercials; so they used one pair of flats and the other was a pair of heels. In the commercial, the transition between flats to heels was shown using camera tricks (see Figure 2). In this case, I gave students credit for the product concept rather than the actual production of a prototype. For products like the wardrobe and body wash (see Figure 2 and Figure 3), these groups created an actual prototype from scratch.

---

1. Students had been taught how to create and edit video materials in previous class activities, so they already had the skills needed to complete this task.

2. Photoshoots were scheduled at times and dates that did not conflict with regular class hours to follow school policy.

Chapter 13

Figure 2. Examples of product prototype studies

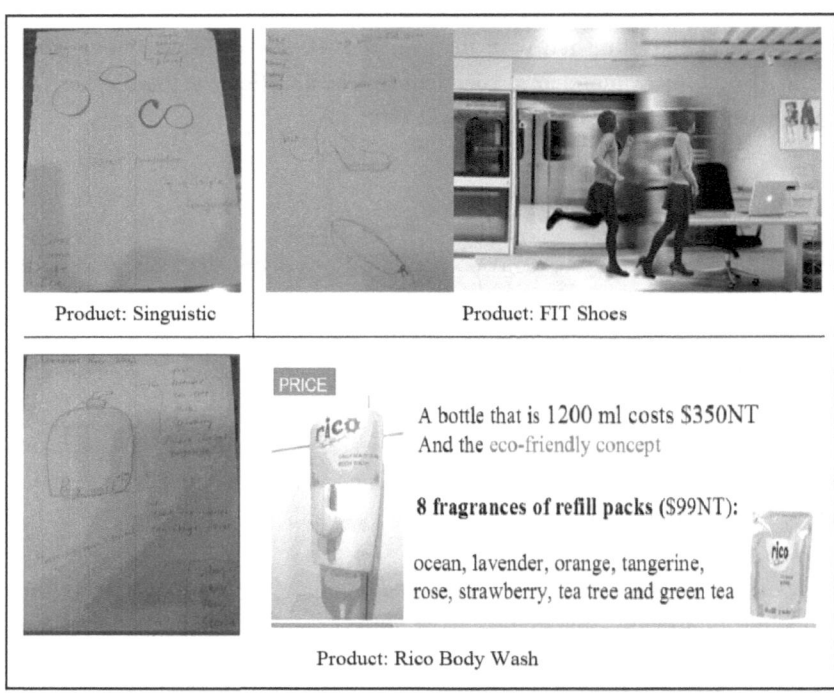

For the rotating wardrobe (see Figure 3), the students made use of cardboard for the wardrobe frames and shelves, and they propped the prototype on top of a rotating dish, inserted two chopsticks on both sides that served as handles for easy rotation. While one rotated the dish, the other shot the video using her mobile device. The voice over used in the ads was also recorded using the same mobile device. For the commercial, they had three different location shoots; all were shot at their respective homes. There were three scenes in the ad. The first one showed a disorganised closet, the other showed a student having problems rummaging through chests looking for appropriate clothing, and the third scene featured a mother having problems putting away her child's clothing as the seasons change. All these scenes portrayed a classic storage problem, and how Magic Wardrobe provides a practical solution. I gave this group extra points for effort and resourcefulness. Creating the cardboard-wardrobe took a lot of time to finish, and the tiny felt paper-doll clothes were actually sewn by hand. This suggests that they put a lot of thought into this project. They also submitted a separate video showing the making of their commercial (Figure 3). In that video, the smiles on their faces, the laughter, and the camaraderie show not only their willingness to do the project but also the fun they had while doing it.

Figure 3. The making of Magic Wardrobe prototype

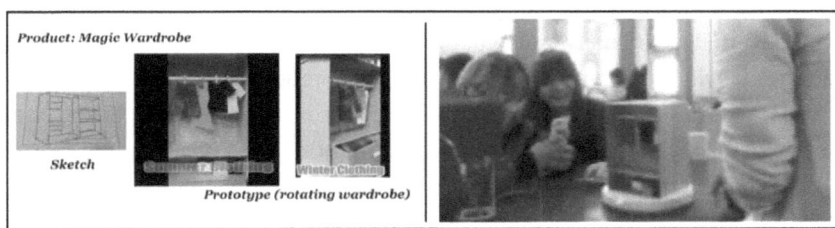

3.4. Oral presentations

Group oral presentations were done on the fourth and fifth week. Each group (four to six students) were given 20 minutes each to present their product development studies. They also had to talk about their individual roles in the project and discuss their work distribution, i.e. who did what and how. This is important to teach students about individual and team responsibility and accountability. They were also required to submit a digital copy of their ads and presentation materials.

3.5. Assessment

The students were assessed using a self-designed rubric, which lists all the requirements that they needed to submit to show completion of the project. I included a scoring scale (1-5) to indicate the quality of work. However, I believe that the assessment sheet needs to incorporate a description of different levels of competence. The performance descriptors with assigned scoring scales would provide a better evaluation for the quality of their work (Efron & Ravid, 2013).

4. Discussion

In addition to the effective integration of technology, this simulation mirrors a real world task that involves the practice of interpersonal communication skills (Crookall & Oxford, 1990). The culmination of the task was an oral presentation where the students showcased a prototype of their product design and TV and print advertising. In many ways, the formal product presentation replicates the scenario in which students will have to use the appropriate language (Littlejohn, 1990) in a business meeting where their ideas and/or proposals are to be vetted by corporate managers. Students presented their product plan providing a rationale for its production, comparative pricing, consumer needs, ads and promotion, etc.

They also provided a run-down of who did what and the difficulties they encountered during production. Some commented that they enjoyed the learning experience but the time involved posed some challenges. I realised that similar to real-life marketing scenarios, the crucial element was shooting and editing the videos and the making of the product prototype. More in-class time should have been spent in a computer lab so students could work on editing and prototype production while I guided and supervised. Nonetheless, they were able to overcome those challenges and their product studies showed their flair for creativity and ingenuity.

This project was collaborative in nature, therefore, it also reinforced the students' team-work skills, and in the process they learned how to share ideas and cultivated their interpersonal competence, all of which has the potential to influence group dynamics. Students had to learn how to adapt and figure out a way to collaborate effectively, to share responsibility and coexist (VanDerPloeg, 2012). Learning to communicate very well helps students to learn respect as they listen to others, and it also teaches them to be supportive and also share and contribute their ideas.

5. Conclusion

By the end of this project, the students had exhibited their knowledge and skills in creating and selling a product. Comprehension of what customer satisfaction entails is crucial in clearly defining what kinds of defects existing products have and how their improved product alleviates those problems. Students had to show how their advertising message is going to stand out in the competition for consumer attention. The merging of traditional and digital ways of presenting creative studies communicates an interesting visual experience that encapsulates relevant ad messages and visual designs in an effective interplay of text, sound (music and voice over), images and videos.

In conclusion, I believe that technology-enhanced collaborative projects, although they require planning and effective time management skills, can reinforce the development of transferable skills in a fun learning environment. The positive learning experience they had in doing this project was the added value that my students got from this course more than what they can get from books alone.

Reference

Crookall, D., & Oxford, R. L. (Eds). (1990). *Simulation, gaming, and language learning.* New York: Newbury House.

Efron, S. E., & Ravid, R. (2013). *Action in research education: A practical guide.* New York: The Guilford Press.

Littlejohn, A. (1990). Testing: The use of simulation/games as a language testing device. In D. Crookall & R. L. Oxford (Eds), *Simulation, gaming and language learning.* New York: Newbury House.

VanDerPloeg, L. S. (2012). *Literacy for a better world: The promise of teaching in diverse classroom.* New York: Teachers College Press.

14. Using Blackboard Wiki pages as a shared space for simulating the professional translation work environment

Juliet Vine[1]

Abstract

The Work-Integrated Simulation for Translators module is part of a three year undergraduate degree in translation. The semester long module aims to simulate several aspects of the translation process using the Blackboard virtual learning environment's Wikis as the interface for completing translation tasks. For each translation task, one of the students is the translator and the other student is the reviser and evaluator. The Source Text (ST) is sent to the students with a translation brief, and they have to co-ordinate between themselves via the Wiki to ensure the whole task is completed within one week. The feedback from the language tutor is also uploaded onto the Wiki, so that both students are able to access the feedback on all parts of the task. The students are also required to reflect on the experience through the journals tool in Blackboard.

Keywords: wiki, translator training, translator competences, procedural knowledge, pair work, reflection.

1. Context/rationale

Translation is the "prototypical teleworking profession" (Olvera-Lobo, 2007, p. 518) and the vast majority of professional translations are completed using information and communication technology (ICT), so it is essential that as part

---

[1]. University of Westminster, United Kingdom; vinej@westminster.ac.uk.

How to cite this chapter: Vine, J. (2015). Using Blackboard Wiki pages as a shared space for simulating the professional translation work environment. In K. Borthwick, E. Corradini, & A. Dickens (Eds), *10 years of the LLAS elearning symposium: Case studies in good practice* (pp. 163-172). Dublin: Research-publishing.net. doi:10.14705/rpnet.2015.000276

of the student's training, they are required to use ICT to complete translation tasks. However, in the module in this case study, gaining confidence in using ICT applications is only one of the aims and objectives. The use of the ICT applications provides the platform for allowing collaborative work and it is through the process of collaboration that students develop the other skills which will be needed in professional translation contexts.

Translation is a complex activity that requires the negotiation of various skills or competences. There has been a long debate about what these skills are and various models of translation competence have been proposed. The PACTE (2003) research group[1] whose main research focus is the acquisition of translation skills has proposed a model of translation competence which consists of six subcategories:

- bilingual;

- extra-linguistic, i.e. knowledge about the world;

- instrumental knowledge about use of documentation;

- ICT, dictionaries, etc;

- transfer, which is the central competence which regulates the other to allow completion of a translation;

- strategic sub-competence, which relates to all the strategies that a translator employs both consciously and subconsciously to resolve translation problems, and psycho-physiological sub-competence, which relates to the psychological attributes required to complete translation tasks.

---

1. PACTE is a research group based at the Universitat Autonoma de Barcelona. The principle researcher is Amparo Hurtado Albir. The group was formed in 1997 and its main research interests are empirical and experimental-based research on translator competence and also translator training.

Of these sub-competences the last four are all related to procedural knowledge, i.e. knowledge of how things happen which can only be gained effectively through doing. So when considering how to train translators, it is important to give students the opportunities to develop these sub-competences. Using ICT in this module not only ensures that students develop the instrumental sub-competence, but also develop the other sub-competences necessary to become professional translators.

2. Aims and objectives

The module aims to provide the opportunity for students to develop skills and knowledge, which ensures that they understand and are able to explicitly address the different translator competences described above, through teleworking in pairs via a Wiki site to accomplish translation tasks.

They develop instrumental skills by using the tools of translation to complete the tasks such as Wikis, internet research, dictionaries, parallel texts and the in-house style guide provided in the introductory sessions.

Transfer competence is developed by working on all the stages that need to be fulfilled to complete the task, e.g. deciding on what translation tools to use, co-ordinating work between the pairs, communicating clearly, and engaging in revision.

Strategic competence is developed by introducing them via the activity to the various strategies necessary to complete the translation according to the brief provided. The use of reflection, which asks students to explicitly think of strategies for dealing with problems that arise out of the translation task, also develops this competence.

Psycho-physiological competences are developed by allowing the students to complete the tasks by the deadline in any manner they decide, so they must be self-motivated, organised and able to manage their time effectively. The

Chapter 14

challenges of relying on others to complete a task and working together are also part of this competence. The use of reflection to underline and reinforce the learning can also be seen as a development within this competence.

3. What I did: the translation task design

In order to clearly explain the module, I will divide this section into three parts: an overview of the whole module in which the translation tasks are set, an introduction to Wikis, and the translation tasks.

3.1. Overview of the module

The module is designed to introduce the students to the professional contexts and practices of the translation industry. This is achieved through the students engaging in the translation tasks and also through a series of talks by guest speakers who introduce their jobs or companies. Each translation task is undertaken by two students: one working as a translator and the other as a reviser/evaluator. A ST with a translation brief is uploaded by the tutor to the blackboard site. The students then have one week to complete the translation and revision using the Wiki to communicate with each other and store documents. Student one uploads the ST to the Wiki and using a word document creates a translation (TT), which once completed is uploaded onto the Wiki. Then student two is able to download the TT, revise it and also evaluate it by filling out a feedback form. The revision and the evaluation are then uploaded to the Wiki. Then student one has an opportunity to comment on the revisions and the evaluation within the Wiki site. The tutor then uploads feedback on the original translation, the revision and the peer evaluation to the Wiki page, so that both students have access to all the feedback. Another important part of the module is introducing reflective practice as part of continuing professional development and as a way of embedding the experiential learning gained through performing the translation tasks. The students are assessed on a portfolio of four translations which they have either translated or revised and evaluated. They are also assessed on a reflective report they write about the module and challenges they faced and the strategies they developed to deal with these challenges.

3.2. Wikis for teaching

Wikis can be found on most virtual learning environments (VLEs). They are a series of webpages that can be modified by anyone who has been given access to them, and changes are tracked: "wikis provide a medium for storing, organising and reformulating the ideas that are contributed by each member of a community" (Carr, 2008, p. 148).

In order to use Wikis on this module, I had to set up groups/pairs of students in the module Blackboard site. The groups/pairs would have exclusive access to their Wiki. We discovered that it was not possible to copy and paste documents directly on to the Wiki page as the formatting of the text became corrupted by the difference between the word documents and the Wiki site. All the documents relating to the translation task were, thus, uploaded as links on the Wiki page according to a set of instructions indicating how they should be named. The Blackboard interface sometimes reacted against documents containing Asian characters and/or numbers which, as a consequence, could not be downloaded and opened from the site. Following the instructions on naming documents and uploading them correctly is part of the task. These actions were assessed under 'professionalism'. Each new translation task can be stored in the same Wiki site on new pages. The Wikis have a comment facility which means that students and tutors can communicate about the task on the page itself, making communication clear and explicit. The tutor is able to assess whether the students have communicated clearly, in a timely fashion and in a professionally appropriate register, and this again is part of the assessment criteria.

3.3. The translation tasks

The module is taught to all students of translation and so has both native and non-native speakers of French, Spanish, German and Chinese. Students are divided up alphabetically into pairs with the same language combination regardless of whether they are native or non-native speakers. The rationale underpinning this decision is that while within professional contexts the best practice is to work into the L1 (i.e. the native language), translators are often asked to revise work in languages they do not speak, in fact in some countries translators may even translate from L1 into L2.

In the introductory sessions, the students are introduced to the translation scenario. It is explained that they are either a free-lance translator working for a translation company or an in-house reviser. The project manager of the translation company sends a source text with a translation brief. The free-lancer then translates it and uploads it to the company website, where the in-house translator revises the translation and also provides feedback on the translation quality. The translator will be sent the revisions for any comments they wish to make about the choices made during the translation process. The project manager then receives the original translation, the revision and the feedback form. The roles are alternated with each translation task.

By the end of the module, each student will have compiled an e-portfolio of four translation tasks. The portfolio includes a translation of L1 to L2 text, a revision of a peer's translation of a L1 to L2 text, a translation of L2 to L1 text and a revision of a peer's translation of a L2 to L1 text. As well as revising the peer's translation, the student must provide feedback on the quality of the translation and award it a mark. The reviser's evaluation and feedback form part of the assessment. Students are also given two shorter texts through which they familiarise with the practical aspects of the task, such as using Wiki pages.

The texts for translation are chosen by the individual language tutors. There is a team meeting of the tutors to co-ordinate the types of texts used across all the languages. All texts should provide translation and revision issues such as formatting issues, as well as extra-linguistic knowledge issues which will require researching. The texts are 300 words long. All texts are provided with a detailed translation brief.

The translation and revision task should be completed within one week of the source text being posted on the Blackboard module site. This tight deadline creates an added pressure on the students to co-ordinate effectively in order not to miss the deadline. Translating under a time constraint is an important aspect of the professional environment and requires students to deal with time-management.

The professional translation competences are explicitly assessed against grading criteria. Professionalism relates to clear and effective communication between all parties, using appropriate language to provide feedback and corrections, finishing the tasks by the deadline, and following procedures accurately. The students are also assessed for translating according to the brief and for their bilingual skills.

4. Discussion: issues arising from running the module

From the student's perspective, the module is very popular. They feel that the translation tasks give them real insight into what might be expected of them in the professional environment. They often feel they have learnt useful skills in working with others, such as communication and time-management, and improved their instrumental skills. Here are two quotes taken from the student's reflective logs:

> "This module helped me practice skills that would not only be crucial in my professional life but also in my day to day life: communication, teamwork, punctuality, diplomacy and most importantly professionalism".

> "As a future translator, it is unequivocal that I have benefited significantly from this module. The module is different from the courses I have taken in my home university in Beijing. What I have learnt in this module has given me a clearer and more realistic perception of how the translation industry runs".

Chapter 14

These very same positives elements also provide the students with some of their greatest challenges. The students worry that their pair work peer will not complete their own tasks on time. They also find it very difficult to evaluate their peers, especially if they feel the language direction of the translation is not their own L2 to L1. However difficult, these challenges are valuable sources of the learning experience, and are often the subject of their reflective logs. It is also important to have contingency plans for when things do go wrong, to reassure students that they will not be penalised for their peer's non-performance.

The module delivery is quite complex and indeed this could be one of its drawbacks, as it does require a lot of explanation to the students at the beginning of the module and in fact two sessions are devoted to this. This can be problematic as the students can feel overwhelmed at the amount of information and all the new technical skills they need to master. This difficulty can be ameliorated by ensuring that information is given in a staged manner and that all the instructions are clear and that there is plenty of opportunity to practice in class and in the first weeks of term. I believe that this complexity of process can be justified within the aims and objectives of this module as it is something students will be expected to deal with in professional contexts when they are introduced to the in-house translation procedures and the in-house styles of their client agencies. It is explained to the students that following the procedures is an important part of the translation task, and will reflect on their professionalism.

As we, the staff group, have learnt more about the quirks of the Wikis, i.e. not recognising and being able to open documents with numbers or characters other than the Roman alphabet and the limitation of not being able to cut and paste onto the Wiki page, there are very few problems with using the Wikis. The students have an opportunity to practice using the system at the beginning of the semester in the in-class workshop and then with the practice tasks.

The module is run across several languages and each language has two language specific translation tutors to provide texts and feedback. The detailed marking of each aspect of the translation task means the tutors are required to mark and add suggested corrections to both the translation and the revision, and to evaluate the peer's feedback. This is very time consuming and with large groups may not be practical. The numbers of tutors working on the module makes it quite complex to administrate and quite expensive to run from the department head's perspective.

The university is redesigning modules to fit in with a new model of teaching which has been called *learning futures*. An important aspect of this is trying to assess the students across the modules, i.e. have less assessment attached to a single module, but find ways to assess students combining the learning from more than one module in one assessment. One of the reasons for this is to take the emphasis off the assessments and shift it to the learning process. In this new system and in fact even in the present system, the module is very intensively assessed which has implications for the student's workload and also for staffing costs. It is possible that these task-based translations using Wikis could be incorporated into the language specific translation classes and the translations could also contain a reflective element. It is also possible that this module could become part of a larger assessment strand focusing on the translation profession and employability.

5. Conclusion

The Wikis in the Blackboard virtual learning environment provide a very effective platform for carrying out the collaborative translation tasks which simulate many aspects of the professional translation industry. Many of the skills acquired through collaborative learning, such as clear communication and effective critical evaluation, are transferrable to other employment situations. The tasks could be designed to incorporate more aspects of a translation task, i.e. by using the Wikis to store glossaries and parallel texts. The students feel the module provides a new and engaging look at professional translation and they feel they learn a lot from completing it. I will finish with a quote from a student's reflective log, where she concludes:

> "The outcome makes me happy and motivates me to pursue my studies further. Also regarding real work life, I gained self-confidence and can see myself working as a translator or interpreter".

References

Carr, N. (2008). Wikis, knowledge building communities and authentic pedagogies in pre-service teacher education. In *Hello! Where are you in the landscape of educational technology? Proceedings ascilite Melbourne 2008* (pp. 147-151). Retrieved from http://www.ascilite.org.au/conferences/melbourne08/procs/carr-n.pdf

Olvera-Lobo, M. D. et al. (2007). A professional approach to translator training (PATT). *Meta: Translators' Journal, 52*(3), 517-528. doi:10.7202/016736ar

PACTE. (2003). Building a translation competence model. In F. Alves (Ed.), T*riangulating translation: Perspectives in process oriented research* (pp. 43-66). Amsterdam: John Benjamins. doi:10.1075/btl.45

Section 4.

New tools, new practices

15 Connected language learning: A tutor's perspective

Benoît Guilbaud[1]

---

1. How did you become interested in using technology in your professional life?

My professional interest in digital technology stemmed from a long-lasting personal interest in the subject. I was fortunate enough to grow up in a family that could be described as 'early adopters' and started playing and creating digitally at a rather early age. While my formal education was overwhelmingly 'chalk and talk', digital technology was omnipresent in my personal life the entire time. Informally, I learnt word-processing, some audio and video editing, and some basic graphic and web design skills.

Later when I studied for my teacher training, I often opted for the technology-oriented modules, seminars or assignment topics that were available. I enjoyed this greatly as I was able to put into practice the skills and knowledge which I had acquired by myself over the years and which I now felt benefited my creativity and personal productivity greatly. It also gave me a feeling of belonging to a group of people sharing a common interest, which was very motivating. In a way, this was my first professional experience of being part of a learning community.

When I began to teach, once again it felt natural to use in my practice the tools I had been using for myself for some time. Creating different document layouts was something I was confident with, as I had been doing it when designing comic strips as a teenager. Furthermore, the skills I learnt recording music as a

---

1. University of Manchester, United Kingdom; benoit.guilbaud@manchester.ac.uk.

How to cite this chapter: Guilbaud, B. (2015). Connected language learning: A tutor's perspective. In K. Borthwick, E. Corradini, & A. Dickens (Eds), *10 years of the LLAS elearning symposium: Case studies in good practice* (pp. 175-184). Dublin: Research-publishing.net. doi:10.14705/rpnet.2015.000277

twenty-something were applied to the way I approached recording and editing listening examinations. Lastly, the skills I had acquired developing my personal website helped me create online resources for Virtual Learning Environments (VLEs).

2. How has your use and knowledge of technology in language learning and teaching developed over time?

In my early career, my use of digital technology was influenced by the functional approach favoured during my teacher training, consisting of teaching IT skills as one of the key skills, alongside numeracy and literacy, and aimed at equipping learners with practical skills they could later reuse in their personal and professional lives. This approach focuses heavily on students acquiring a general fluency and comfort in navigating around and using a computer, which Warschauer (2003) identifies as the most basic component of digital literacy. It allows learners to familiarise themselves with the tools used in class, such as an interactive whiteboard, or outside the class, such as a VLE, but this contact with technology remains for the most part passive (e.g. accessing documents) and very controlled (e.g. writing a few words on the interactive whiteboard).

However, as my practice developed, using this approach to technology began to feel like I was superimposing new tools on a traditional teaching model. Little use was made of the affordances of networked technologies. The short pieces students wrote on the VLE could have well been written on paper, and pair work in the language lab seemed to offer little benefit, if any, over face-to-face interaction.

Overall, I often felt that I was only using technology for an added motivation bonus, or even just sometimes for the sake of it. From there, my views began to change as I started considering how networked technologies could help define the way I should approach my teaching.

3. How has contact with colleagues impacted on the way you use technology in language learning and teaching?

Since I began teaching French language in higher education, I have been fortunate enough to attend a number of conferences to help develop my practice.

After attending the LLAS e-learning symposium in 2013, I wrote a blog post entitled 'A sense of community', in which I described how the event made me feel like I belonged to a group (Guilbaud, 2013). I felt useful and engaged, and was able to make connections. I later realised how this echoed what McMillan and Chavis (1986) identify as the four criteria defining a learning community: membership, influence, fulfilment of individual needs and shared events of emotional connections. The fellow practitioners I have met at this event have been a tremendous help in developing my practice, acting as a sounding board, suggesting ideas, praising or critiquing my work and views.

4. How do you use technology in your professional practice now?

The ways I use technology in my professional practice can be broadly divided into two categories, depending on whether I use them for teaching or for my own professional development. Firstly, I use the following tools in my teaching practice:

- digital resources: most of the resources I use are digital or digitised. I enjoy the duplicability this affords and I normally make all resources (AV, hand-outs) available to my students after class. It has been argued that giving away all class materials can discourage attendance, however this has not been the case in my experience;

- my personal laptop: I rarely teach a class without it. I particularly like the predictability associated with using my own computer. Audio-visual materials always look the way they were meant too, and I can use a variety of software packages which do not come as standard on institutional machines: contextual dictionaries (defining words directly from any document or web page), my French dictionary (I use the digital edition of *Le Petit Robert 2011* and prefer it to most free online platforms), some mind-mapping and presentation software (MindNode Pro, Keynote). It also saves me several minutes a day from logging to various web services;

- online platforms and software: vocabulary apps (Quizlet), online dictionaries (WordReference.com, Linguee.fr), text-to-speech software, dictation software, audio and video capture software (Camtasia, WM Capture, Audio Hijack Pro);

- communication tools: discussion forums and collaborative documents (Google Drive), some web 2.0 platforms (Ning, Quizlet).

Secondly, these are the tools I frequently use in order to further my professional development:

- the web 2.0 platform Twitter has had a tremendous impact on my professional life. I will return to this in the next section of this article;

- I also use a number of other social platforms in my professional life including WordPress (for hosting my blog), Flickr (for finding and sharing pictures on Creative Commons licences) and SlideShare (for posting and embedding slides from presentations I give).

5. How does your knowledge and experience in social media and web 2.0 technologies impact on your professional and teaching life?

Social media and web 2.0 technologies have had a significant impact on my teaching practice over the past few years. Whilst my interest in technology in general has contributed to shape my teaching on a practical level, social media and web 2.0 technologies, or networked technologies as I will refer to them, have had a more profound impact on how I perceive my role as an educator and how I go about performing this role. In this section, I will outline how the growing importance of networked technologies in my professional life has informed and influenced my teaching.

5.1. From Twitter user to life-long learner

The best example of the influence of web 2.0 technologies on my professional development is how I became a Twitter user. I joined Twitter in 2010 but didn't really use or see the point of this platform for about a year. In 2011, I attended two conferences, the 7th LLAS e-learning Symposium in Southampton and the 6th International Conference "Education in a Changing Environment: Creativity and Engagement in Higher Education" in Salford. At these conferences, for the first time, I saw Twitter being used for a constructive purpose: it allowed delegates to communicate among themselves, comment on the talks and easily access slides and resources from the presentations they had missed. Several 'tweet walls' were up and displaying thoughts and comments that speakers and delegates had been posting throughout the conference. I felt really engaged in the intellectual discussions taking place during these events, and I have been using Twitter ever since to share my own thoughts and views on the language teaching profession as well as various intellectual issues. I have shared and accessed teaching resources, made connections with fellow practitioners, some of which I later had the pleasure to meet and work with in person.

I now endeavour to maintain and develop my Personal Learning Network (PLN) (Couros, 2010). A PLN can be defined as an ensemble of connections, people and tools (web 2.0 platforms for the most part) which a person can draw upon for intellectual and professional development. Networked practitioners communicate and collaborate through the medium of their PLNs. In order to maintain a healthy give-and-take relationship with the learning community formed by my PLN, I have chosen to share some of the information I access,

Chapter 15

curate or produce: I regularly post my presentations on SlideShare, I post links to my readings on Twitter, and I share tips and teaching resources on my WordPress blog, or occasionally on community platforms such as humbox. ac.uk.

As part of this process, I have developed a semi-public online identity. This process can be challenging as it implies letting go of some of the control that one would naturally try and retain in terms of privacy or intellectual property. Constructing a digital identity took time and effort but it has benefited me greatly. More than a technique or a means to an end, this approach to learning, networked learning (Couros, 2011), has been a way to further my own intellectual development as a life-long learner.

5.2. Teaching principles: from constructivism to connectivism

My training as a language tutor was largely influenced by constructivist learning theories, which pose knowledge as a social construction generated, in part, by learners through their interactions with each other. In concrete terms, this means that students learn to use the language with the assistance of their peers and tutor, as well as class materials and self-study materials in the library. For the sake of this argument, I will compare Vygotsky's (1978) zone of proximal development to a local network. In this network, students establish connections with the people and resources that are physically present. Some of the knowledge acquired through these connections can persist beyond the classroom (e.g. through class notes) but some of it will no longer be accessible once the class has ended.

Connectivist learning theories (Siemens, 2005) build upon these constructivist principles and suggest that using networked technologies, such as web 2.0 and social media, allows learners to expand on their zone of proximal development. By making and sustaining connections outside the classroom, students become more independent learners. By developing their own PLNs, they can make connections to wider learning communities. They can select and share with others resources representing an interest to their own learning, and access and evaluate those shared by others in order to gradually develop more independent learning habits.

Connectivist learning theories argue that the connections created by a learner are more valuable than the resulting knowledge. It's not about possessing information, it's about knowing how and where to find information. Making connections can help learners become much more resourceful, keep their knowledge current and relevant and face new learning challenges with greater ease. It can be argued that this approach to learning is particularly relevant in the current economic climate, where change management and adaptability are seen as core skills to secure employment.

5.3. Learning in the open: the example of discussion forums for translation

In order to explain how these principles have influenced my teaching, I will first draw upon an example from a translation class which I taught for several years. I initially recommended to my students to use offline and online dictionaries, including the translation website and discussion forum WordReference.com. The discussions found on the website offer a lot of value over regular dictionaries in terms of contextualisation and semantic disambiguation. When we discussed the possibility of students contributing to these forums, everyone agreed that they were very useful, yet few seemed willing to take the plunge and participate to public online discussions, mainly for lack of confidence in their language skills.

In order to take steps towards addressing this issue, I decided to start weekly discussions around the translation homework using a web 2.0 platform, Ning.com. Without being public, this platform was open to all students currently enrolled on the degree programme. The learning community was therefore potentially much larger than the translation class itself. All content would also be preserved over time, unlike on the VLE's discussion boards, which would get reset every academic year. The uptake for this new platform was good and some very constructive discussions took place around the homework, and over time students became more confident in sharing and critiquing not only part of their work, but also the resources they had used.

Using these semi-open discussion forums was a modest but arguably successful first step in encouraging my students to establish two-way connections with a learning community wider than their classroom, and to take an active role in their learning process by producing content and offering suggestions on other learners' content. I later had the pleasure to see that one of my students had gone and posted a very useful contribution on the forums of WordReference.com.

5.4. Learning as a participatory process: the example of collaborative vocabulary lists

In order to further illustrate the benefits and risks associated with connectivism in language teaching and learning, I will take the example of the collaborative vocabulary application Quizlet.com, which I recently started using in my teaching practice.

Two years ago, I started looking for a new way for students to study vocabulary. I have taught on specialist language courses including medical and business French, and whilst the specificity of this type of language teaching extends beyond the lexical element, vocabulary learning remains a central part of it. I wanted to find a way for students to be engaged with their learning process and participate in the design of the materials rather than to be memorising vocabulary lists that would be provided to them.

Someone in my PLN recommended Quizlet.com. The specificity of this platform is that user-generated vocabulary lists are available publicly on the website. I thought it would be interesting if our students collaboratively compiled vocabulary lists relating to their weekly course topics and made them available on the internet for other medical students potentially interested in learning

French. So a system was set in place for students from a few different classes to collaboratively generate, as homework, their own online vocabulary lists. Every week, each student added five words to a list on a given topic. Once proofread and curated by the course tutors, these lists were made available on Quizlet for our students, and many others, to learn from.

This approach helped our students get in the drivers' seat. They now had to decide which words or phrases would be the most useful to them, depending on the context. It took a few weeks for each class to fine tune the length, format and content of their lists but the overall results were very satisfactory. A survey carried out at the end of the semester showed that students were very pleased that they created and shared what was, in fact, an open educational resource. Most agreed that the result of the common effort was better than what each of them could have produced on their own. Overall, this was a fruitful learning experience.

However, contrary to expectations, letting students write their own vocabulary lists did not lighten the burden placed on the tutor, but rather shifted it. Correcting entries proved a very time-consuming task, along with chasing late contributions and removing duplicates. Curating content requiring specialist knowledge (particularly in the case of medical French) was also challenging at times.

This echoes some of the issues which may be encountered in a communicative language teaching context. In this configuration, the tutor becomes a facilitator and curator of knowledge rather than a dispenser of content. Some tutors may find this change of situation threatening or stressful, and may be reluctant to relinquish control over their classroom. I would argue that enabling learners to complete tasks semi-autonomously and letting them take charge of their learning process is valuable and worth the risk. An individual contribution of five words per week to a list is a small step, but the fact that the rest of the group, as well as many other learners on the internet may potentially be learning these five words should hopefully encourage our students to engage with their own learning on a scale greater than that within the classroom walls.

5.5. Conclusion

Through these examples, I have reflected upon the impact that networked technologies have had on my professional life and teaching practice. Using these tools has undoubtedly helped shape the way I look at my own professional development and they have certainly contributed to the fact that I view myself as a life-long learner. My online participation, modest as it may be, is an act of civic engagement and social responsibility. Engaging with learning communities on a give-and-take basis is an ethic which, as a teacher, I feel I must transmit to my students, to help them embrace participation over consumption, and become life-long learners –of French, preferably.

References

Couros, A. (2010). Developing personal learning networks for open and social learning. In G. Veletsianos (Ed.), *Emerging technologies in distance education*. Athabasca University Press.

Couros, A. (2011). Why networked learning matters. Presented at *Education in a Changing Environment (ECE) 6th International Conference, Creativity and Engagement in Higher Education, 6-8 July 2011, University of Salford, Greater Manchester, UK*.

Guilbaud, B. (2013, January 26). LLAS e-learning symposium 2013 pt1: A sense of community. *Benoît Guilbaud's Web blog*. Retrieved from http://benguilbaud.com/2013/01/26/llas-e-learning-symposium-2013-pt1-a-sense-of-community/

McMillan, D. W., & Chavis, D. M., (1986). Sense of community: A definition and theory. *Journal of Community Psychology, 14*(1), 6-23.

Siemens, G. (2005). Connectivism: A learning theory for the digital age. *International Journal of Instructional Technology & Distance Learning, 2*(1). Retrieved from http://itdl.org/journal/jan_05/article01.htm

Vygotsky, L. S. (1978). *Mind in society: The development of higher mental processes*. Cambridge, MA: Harvard University Press.

Warschauer, M. (2003). *Technology and social inclusion: Rethinking the digital divide*. Cambridge, MA: MIT Press.

16. The e-learning tool Voxopop and its benefits on oral skills: Activities for final year students of German

Sascha Stollhans[1]

Abstract

This case study demonstrates how Voxopop, a voice based e-learning tool, can be used to practise oal skills in the target language by presenting activities which have been developed for students of German at the University of Nottingham. The focus lies on an ongoing innovative project designed to improve final year students' oral skills by having them interact with each other on Voxopop, specifically in the context of debriefing them on their year abroad experience. Like many Internet forums, Voxopop is a platform to exchange ideas and engage in discussions. However, this is done in oral instead of written form and is therefore an opportunity to practise oral performances in the target language. The key advantage of Voxopop lies in the fact that it is self-explanatory, user-friendly and accessible online so students can use it anywhere, with minimal equipment (e.g. their laptop or smartphone). It creates an environment where students do not feel under pressure as they can practise, listen back and re-record themselves before uploading their contributions. This also gives students the opportunity to reflect on their own output and find out about their strengths and weaknesses when producing the target language orally.

Keywords: oral skills, collaborative dialogue, year abroad, autonomous learning, self-reflection, e-learning, online discussion.

---

1. The University of Nottingham, Nottingham, United Kingdom; Sascha.Stollhans@nottingham.ac.uk.

How to cite this chapter: Stollhans, S. (2015). The e-learning tool Voxopop and its benefits on oral skills: Activities for final year students of German. In K. Borthwick, E. Corradini, & A. Dickens (Eds), *10 years of the LLAS elearning symposium: Case studies in good practice* (pp. 185-192). Dublin: Research-publishing.net. doi:10.14705/rpnet.2015.000278

1. Context/rationale

"One learns to speak by speaking" (Swain, 1985, p. 248). This statement by second language acquisition researcher Merrill Swain might be controversial, it is, however, arguable that producing the target language is an essential part of the language learning process. Swain (1985) further explains that "producing the target language may be the trigger that forces the learner to pay attention to the means of expression needed in order to successfully convey his or her own intended meaning" (p. 249). This idea forms the basis of the *Comprehensible Output Hypothesis*, one of the main theories of language acquisition.

There is much debate in second language acquisition research about how one best acquires languages, and also about how fluency and accuracy in the target language should be evaluated in the context of real-world language use. Language teachers will find that oral skills in the target language are highly important to their students. Many students ask for more opportunities to improve their oral performance in terms of grammatical accuracy, pronunciation and fluency. Often they feel that after their year abroad they have become much more fluent, but they still find themselves making the same mistakes repeatedly, sometimes without even noticing them.

Whereas more and more educationalists see the benefits of technology enhanced language learning, and computer assisted teaching and learning is not foreign to language classrooms in the UK anymore, technology is hardly ever used to actively focus on productive skills. "Foreign language (FL) teachers have always been ahead of the curve in integrating technology in FL instruction and learning, seeing the benefits of technology" (LeLoup & Ponterio, 2003, para 1), but according to Sharma (2009), "the influence of technology on the productive skills of speaking and writing is, arguably, less. If you wish to improve fluency, many students would argue that nothing is better than a face-to-face language lesson, a discussion class with the teacher" (para 10).

This case study presents an innovative project which tries to fill this gap by providing opportunities for students to work independently on their oral skills and to reflect on and evaluate their own output in the target language. It uses Voxopop, a voice based e-learning tool which facilitates recording online discussions. Voxopop is similar to other common internet forums, it is a platform to exchange ideas and engage in discussions. However, this is done in oral instead of in written form, and is hence an opportunity to practise oral performances in the target language. The key advantage of Voxopop lies in the fact that it is self-explanatory, user-friendly and accessible online so students can use it anywhere they go, e.g. at home, and with minimal equipment (e.g. their laptop or smartphone). Recordings can be private or restricted and in this safe environment students are not under pressure as they can practise, listen back and re-record themselves before uploading their contributions.

The project described and evaluated in this case study is an ongoing project at the University of Nottingham which allows final year students of German to record themselves speaking about an aspect of their year abroad and to discuss it in a Voxopop talkgroup. This involves listening to other students' contributions online, understanding them and replying to them with another recording.

2. Aims and objectives

The major aim of the project was to give students the opportunity to work on their oral language skills independently and autonomously whilst reflecting on their year abroad experience. Students were asked to record an anecdote from their year abroad, listen to their peers' recordings and comment on them. I anticipated that having to record themselves and being able to redo their recording would encourage students to prepare their oral contributions thoroughly and thus raise their language awareness in terms of accuracy, word choice and pronunciation. This is related to Merrill Swain's ideas about 'collaborative dialogue' and 'metatalk', i.e. opportunities for students to reflect on their own output in the target language collaboratively and maybe even discuss it on a metalinguistic level, which is considered to be highly beneficial to the language learning process (cf. Swain, Brooks, & Tocalli-Beller, 2002).

I also hoped that students would find it useful to share their impressions from their year abroad as well as learn from their fellow students' experiences. Against the background of task-based language learning I tried to create a relatable task, with a real context, to make students feel that what they were going to do had an authentic purpose other than, or in addition to language learning. In general, students both recognise and appreciate the opportunity to use their language skills in a real-life context, rather than a forced, non-contextual scenario.

3. What I did

The project aimed at a cohort of 48 final year students of German within the context of their core language module in the autumn semester of 2013-14. After an introduction to the tool and a practice run which was meant to enable students to familiarise themselves with the tool, they received the following instruction:

> Report on something entertaining/interesting/exciting/sad/... you experienced on your year abroad in a German speaking country (approx. 3 minutes). Record at least five comments or questions as a response to your peers' contributions.

The project revolved around the year abroad because for many students this year marks a professional, linguistic and personal high point of their degree, which they wish and need to discuss and evaluate.

In preparation for the activity, the first thing I had to do was to create a Voxopop talkgroup and invite all students to join by email. I also created a video tutorial with *screencast-o-matic* in which I explained and demonstrated all required steps, from signing up to uploading a contribution and commenting on another contribution. In doing so, I tried to avoid confusion and make it easier for students to focus on the actual task. The talkgroup used for this project was a private talkgroup, i.e. students' recordings were private and only open to their fellow students, who were also invited members.

In the talkgroup, I created a discussion zone for each seminar group as well as two additional discussion zones, one for students to test the various features of the tool and one for them to ask questions and discuss any problems they might find. Each student started a new discussion for their main contribution within their respective discussion zone.

During our mid-term 'Project Week', the students worked on the task. They uploaded a recording of their story, listened to their classmates' stories and commented on them. This resulted in very creative contributions and engaging discussions in the target language. Students shared interesting experiences which were sometimes funny and sometimes sad. Many stories reported on intercultural misunderstandings, new discoveries or unexpected reactions from people the students had met on their year abroad.

4. Discussion

I asked students to fill out a short survey to express their opinion on the project and their perception of its contribution to their language learning success. The majority of students described Voxopop as a "fun tool" and 85% stated that they had enjoyed using it. There were a few comments outlining that it was slightly awkward having to listen to one's own voice and that this was something which students needed to get used to when working with Voxopop for the first time.

All students who took the survey had recorded their contribution more than once, 46% had recorded it twice, and 54% three times or more. This shows that students had taken the opportunity to listen back and re-record themselves, possibly after becoming aware of any grammatical inaccuracies or pronunciation weaknesses. All students *agreed* or *strongly agreed* that "listening back to my recording made me hear/become aware of my own mistakes" and "listening back to my recording made me hear/become aware of my own pronunciation weaknesses", and 84% felt that the activity encouraged them to reflect on various linguistic aspects (e.g. grammar, vocabulary and pronunciation) within the context of oral target language use. This proves the usefulness of such an activity to raise students' language awareness, which is also reflected in the following two instances of collaborative dialogue and metatalk (cf. Swain et al., 2002) from the Voxopop talkgroup:

(1) "That's a great story but what does the expression X mean? - It means something like Y."

(2) "It's cool that you picked up an Austrian accent as well. Have you learned any dialect words? Let's speak Austrian!"

These two extracts from discussions students led on Voxopop focus on the linguistic output itself. The student who commented on the original contribution had picked up on certain aspects of the other student's language and now enquired about them. Working with the tool seems to have encouraged some students to pay close attention to certain linguistic aspects, which is also demonstrated quite clearly by the following two open comments made by students in the survey:

"Listening back to our own recordings makes you realise your own strengths and weaknesses in pronunciation and intonation etc. – we always hear ourselves speak, but never hear how we actually sound to other people, so I found that listening back to recordings was really useful, especially since our oral exams are recorded!"

"In an ordinary conversation I do not analyse in depth every sentence I speak as long as I am capable of getting my point across. While using Voxopop, on the other hand, I had to re-listen to what I said and thus focus on assessing my linguistic strengths or weaknesses. Consequently, it was a great tool which allowed me to improve some of my linguistic mistakes. I wish we had used it more."

In other comments students mentioned that the activity helped them to practise their spoken German and in particular accommodate students who don't feel very comfortable speaking up in class. 92% of the students who took part in the survey agreed that this specific activity was contextually beneficial and that tools such as Voxopop can help them build their speaking confidence.

Some students also commented that they found it useful to listen to contributions from other students as it helped them learn new expressions in context.

The only negative aspect some students mentioned were technical problems they had encountered to begin with. In order to be able to use Voxopop adequately, the latest updates of Flash and Java must be installed. However, those problems could be resolved very quickly, and the Voxopop website contains a very useful section on how to deal with technical difficulties.

5. Conclusion

Overall, the project was very successful. Most students enjoyed working with Voxopop as it boosted their confidence and encouraged them to pay close attention to their own linguistic output when producing the target language orally. It also provided a very valuable self-study opportunity, a way to work on a project collaboratively and, not least, a fun supplement to the regular language classes.

There are plans to expand the project in the future and to integrate Voxopop on a more regular basis into language teaching at all levels, for instance by making it a joint second and final year project related to the year abroad. In this way, second year students who are still to leave for their year abroad could benefit from their fellow students' experience; and fruitful collaboration between students from different stages could be created.

At the moment, we are using Voxopop as a platform to facilitate the linguistic and cultural exchange between some of our second year students and our current Erasmus students from Germany and Austria. I am also looking into other e-learning tools which could be beneficial for oral skills in the target language.

This may be of particular interest to students on the *ab initio* strand who will be integrated with the post A-Level cohort at some point during their degree. That group of students is usually less confident about producing the target language orally and thus may benefit very much from opportunities to work on those skills independently.

References

LeLoup, J. W., & Ponterio, R. (2003). *Second language acquisition and technology: A review of the research*. EDO-FL-03-11.

Sharma, P. (2009, April 8). Controversies in using technology in language teaching. *BBC Teaching English*. Retrieved from http://www.teachingenglish.org.uk/article/controversies-using-technology-language-teaching

Swain, M. (1985). Communicative competence: Some roles of comprehensible input and comprehensible output in its development. In S. M. Gass & C. Madden (Eds), *Input in second language acquisition* (pp. 235-253). Rowley: Newbury House Pub.

Swain, M., Brooks, L., & Tocalli-Beller, A. (2002). Peer-peer dialogue as a means of second language learning. *Annual Review of Applied Linguistics, 22*, 171-185. doi:10.1017/S0267190502000090

Video Tutorial: http://www.youtube.com/watch?v=5VNPO1tK9BQ&feature=youtu.be

Voxopop: www.voxopop.com

17. Sound literature: The pedagogy of reconnection through student-authored audiobooks in the Spanish curriculum

Susana Lorenzo-Zamorano[1]

Abstract

This article is based on a case study I presented at the elearning Symposium 2014 and focuses on an undergraduate project which had received the Teaching Enhancement and Student Success Fund at the University of Manchester two years before. The project was conceived as an outreach activity complementing the final year core language classes and aimed at engaging students with both reading and listening to advanced texts and enjoying literature through weekly reading groups and audiobooks. Ultimately, through reading and creating literature, the objective was to foster students' intercultural competence after the year abroad. It was thus a student-centred and task-orientated project involving the creation of an audiobook by its participants. To this end, different forms of technology were introduced, each serving a particular purpose and fitting into specific learning goals. In this article I will report on the use of tablet PC technology for marking and giving feedback as well as on the benefits of audiobooks for language teaching in the context of higher education, where they have not yet had an extensive use.

Keywords: audiobooks, literature, tablet PC technology, OERs, productive and receptive skills, creativity, student generated content, personalised learning, intercultural competence.

---

1. University of Manchester, United Kingdom; Susana.Lorenzo@manchester.ac.uk.

How to cite this chapter: Lorenzo-Zamorano, S. (2015). Sound literature: The pedagogy of reconnection through student-authored audiobooks in the Spanish curriculum. In K. Borthwick, E. Corradini, & A. Dickens (Eds), *10 years of the LLAS elearning symposium: Case studies in good practice* (pp. 193-202). Dublin: Research-publishing.net. doi:10.14705/rpnet.2015.000279

Chapter 17

1. Context/rationale

Owing to time and content constraints in the language curriculum, literature is only covered fragmentarily inside the classroom and few students take on the task of reading for pleasure. What is more, literature tends to be perceived by them as more complex than other subjects and its connections with other disciplines across the curriculum tend to be overlooked. This perception among learners finds its reflection in what can be argued to be considered a pedagogical gap in the curriculum given the fact that the offer of literature courses has generally narrowed. Referring to the Departments of English in the American context, William M. Chace (2009) maintains that the causes for this decline have to do with a failure to make a strong case to undergraduates that knowledge of literature and the tradition in which it exists is "a human good in and of itself" (para. 5). Our initiative to introduce literature in the format of audiobooks and having students then creating their own audiobooks was indeed an attempt to help reconnect them to both written and aural literature. Another essential element of the rationale for this project was based on students' progress and achievements during their year abroad, which is often considered to be one of the most important experiences for language learners from a linguistic and intercultural point of view. However, in a considerable number of cases, this does not happen automatically for a combination of reasons, such as motivation, learning style and personality, home university accreditation and requirements.

On the other hand, those students who experience an improvement in their oral-aural communication skills do not necessarily show a correlation of the latter with other aspects of language performance such as grammar, writing and (inter)cultural skills. Thus, we set up the project with the primary goal of helping students not only to improve their writing skills but also to support their acquisition of a more comprehensive knowledge and understanding of the Hispanic world.

2. Aims and objectives

- To further enhance the linguistic competence of final year language students.

- To promote advanced literacy and an enjoyment of reading, and help create lifelong readers.

- To facilitate content-area understanding and thus improve students' performance across other departmental course units that focus on Hispanic cultural studies.

- To provide students with a set of transferable skills: critical, intercultural, cognitive and creative, in order to enable them to have a better understanding of the world and enhance their employability.

- To help create a sense of community in a discipline that has a high and increasing student uptake.

- To enhance our students' learning experience by putting them at the centre of their learning and offering them extra support.

3. What we did

The participants were tasked with creating their own audiobook and making it available as downloadable media on our course website. There were three requirements: short stories had to be 500-700 words long, they had to be completely original and include at least one Hispanic component. A short reflective paragraph on the narrative choices made and the motivation of each student was also asked for. In terms of assessment, and with a view to have some minimum recruitment, 10% of the final mark for the course was assigned to this project, more specifically, 5% for the written part and 5% for the oral one.

To be noted is the fact that, through the integration into the short story of at least one Hispanic element, the purpose was to try to measure the impact of study abroad on our students' intercultural skills. More specifically, through students' creative process, we wanted to see the degree of cultural awareness and sensitivity to the target culture which they had acquired during their year abroad. To illustrate this pivotal idea and prepare students to carry out their task, we selected a few short stories from the audiobook collections *Relatos españoles contemporáneos* (de la Flor, 2008), *Relatos del Río de la Plata* (de la Flor & Paúl, 2009), and *Relatos mexicanos* (de la Flor, 2010), making sure they all had a historical and cultural background of Hispanic interest. The selection was also made in terms of language varieties as we wanted to expose students to different accents. After integrating these short stories into our language curriculum, we then created a wider reading/listening schedule for weekly get-together sessions. A few of these weekly sessions were dedicated to pronunciation and fluency as well as to facilitating the understanding of the key elements of short stories in general, i.e. character, setting, plot, conflict, and theme. Finally, students submitted an initial draft of their short story on which substantial feedback was provided before they could submit their final version.

In order to deliver milestones and as a means of communication, the project also involved the use of online technologies, in particular, of some of the standard features in Blackboard such as wikis, voice tools and Turnitin, the latter with the objective of enabling us to detect possible cases of plagiarism and also for administrative purposes, e.g. extension requests. Additionally, to correct and provide feedback on the first draft of the short stories, we decided to use tablet PC technology as we thought it would not only be quicker than other options (GradeMark within Turnitin), but would also provide more of a natural near-pen-and-paper feedback. To this purpose, with a budget of 1000 GBP and some research on the part of a technologist assigned to the project, we were handed two Dell Latitude ST tablet PCs with a 10-inch multi-touch display and a digital pen.

4. Discussion

4.1. Student involvement and measuring success

The degree of success and involvement on the part of the participants was very high. We initially recruited 50 students out of 140 and, although numbers went down as students were made aware of the extra commitment they had to make, we ended up with 35. The success in terms of satisfaction was reflected on the student post-project questionnaires (Figure 1), course unit evaluations and informal correspondence.

Figure 1. Post-project questionnaire results

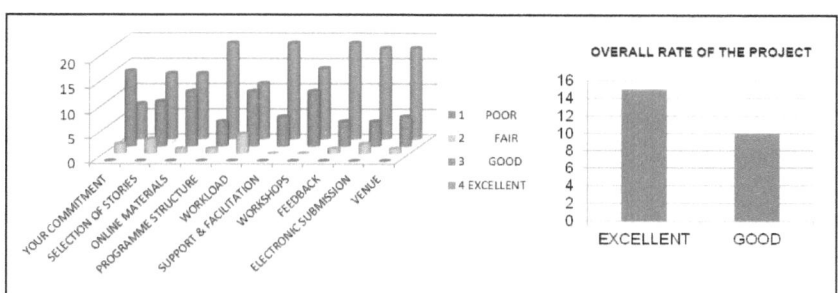

All in all participants valued the extra opportunity to practise creative thinking and writing and improve their oral and aural skills in a more informal atmosphere. One of the outcomes was the creation of a reading community that went beyond the classroom, which was very relevant within the context of the high and increasing student uptake in SPLAS (Spanish, Portuguese and Latin American Studies), and helped us to address the personalised learning agenda which underpinned the Manchester Undergraduate Education Review.

As the project promoted the integration of the main linguistic skills, both receptive (listening, reading) and productive (speaking, writing), it also had a positive impact on students' general performance in language. Although it only contributed 10% to the final mark for the course unit SPLA30210 (final year Spanish language), all participants, except for one, obtained a higher mark in both components of the project than in the written and oral exam of the course, and 7 participants did see an improvement in their oral mark degree classification as a result.

Attendance was very good and participants made regular use of our office hours for informal feedback and consultation, something which was highly valued in the questionnaires. What is more, even after having finished all their exams, students were still willing to provide us with revised recordings of their stories for publication with extra creative enhancements such as original sound effects. The following are some of the students' comments:

> "I loved the audiobooks project. It was touted as a fun extra module that would be beneficial and, although the fun element did disappear quite quickly as the workload came, I really enjoyed the classes and the opportunity to do something creative. Although it was extra work, I'm sure my Spanish has benefitted even a little and I would recommend it to other final year students".

> "I really enjoyed the audiobooks project. It was a great idea and it really helped me with my creative writing and pronunciation".

> "I gained confidence in speaking and writing. It's a good way to get feedback".

> "I would recommend this project because it really helped me with creative writing and I learned some very useful vocabulary that I don't usually come across because I am a MLBM [modern languages and business management] student. My suggestion is having these classes run during the whole year".

> "I would recommend this project but I would warn that writing a story is much harder than I anticipated and that you must be prepared to work hard on the drafts. The tutors were enthusiastic and it was a good opportunity to read Hispanic literature. However, a bit more guidance on the creative side would have helped me".

In terms of student production and from the facilitators' point of view, the success of the project was evident in the final product. A good number of students managed to successfully produce unique narrative structures, engaging plots, and complex characters with very original ideas. From the linguistic point of view, there was a general improvement in the use of syntax and a greater awareness of more complex stylistic issues relating, for example, to Spanish adjective placement. When it came to reading their own short story, students had to concentrate on the prosodic features of the language, i.e. lexical stress, intonation, pronunciation, rhythm and fluency, which gave us an opportunity to assess these elements in very different circumstances than those in which spontaneous speech is produced.

4.2. The use of technology: challenges, benefits and lessons learned

The fact that students did not have to go through the traditional submission process was well received, not to mention the savings in terms of both time and printing. From the students' perspective the use of tablet PCs by the tutors meant that they could access our feedback electronically once we had uploaded the marked short stories to Blackboard.

On the contrary, from the tutors' point of view, getting used to the digital pen was a bit of a challenge requiring some practice before being able to make our writing legible. Therefore, the time dedicated to marking and providing feedback with a tablet PC was far longer than what we had originally planned and, doing it within two weeks, which is the official time to return marked coursework, was only possible thanks to the dedication and hard work of the tutors[1].

One of the main advantages was the fact that we could transfer exactly the same symbol-based marking system we use in class which students are familiar with. The visual element was another advantage as electronic ink can be colour coded and thus we could use different colours and styles of underlining according to the type of error. Additionally, we could make use of other common tools such as 'tracking changes', and it also allowed us to change the font size and line spacing in order to adapt them to our own visual

---

1. I want to take this opportunity to thank both my colleagues Noelia Alcarazo and Oscar Garcia for their invaluable help.

needs. Also on a positive note, the tablets offered us the possibility to insert small comments through Microsoft Word.

I think, however that, we need to be clear about the possible downsides of technology. For example, when it came to giving more substantial feedback, the keyboard on the screen was not the best option for typing and we had to rely on our own PC desktop to add these comments, something which could have been avoided if the tablet had included a USB port to connect a keyboard to it.

It is also worth noting that the speed of the tablet was rather slow. Moreover, we could only use the digital pen on Word documents and not on PDF ones. Another downside was the fact that, once the marking and feedback process had been completed, all these Word documents had to be converted to PDF format before making them available online to students, in order to prevent the correction symbols from moving around.

Finally, although the involvement in the virtual learning environment was not as high as we had expected, our final year language module (SPLA30210) was highly commended in the 2011/12 Best on Blackboard competition, with students making specific comments on the materials and variety of tools made available for the project.

5. Conclusion

The project came to an end with a selection of student-authored short stories being compiled in a special paper publication and disseminated through our Spanish newspaper. What this cohort of students produced is also now available on our final year language course website and forms part of our language curriculum. Thus we pride ourselves in promoting literature through our students' own short stories. However, the amount of work put into the whole creative process both by students and teacher-facilitators sadly outbalances the visibility of the end product and we were indeed very short sighted not to see its wider educational value and potential benefits for other students of Spanish around the world, not to mention its value as a marketing tool for our own institution[1]. We are now in the process of trying to get in touch with the participants in order to get consent for their work to be openly accessible online, but this is not easy considering they graduated two years ago. However, as the project itself has been embedded into the final year language curriculum, we hope to progressively gather a good selection of student-generated content and ultimately create an Open Access Digital Library with their short stories.

All in all, using tablet technology in this project has opened new horizons to us and made us realise that we have only touched the tip of an iceberg that looks promising, as long as technology is embraced in a flexible way and perceived as a means to enhance the student experience and not as an end in itself. It goes without saying that the functionality of Tablet PCs to provide feedback depends greatly on how powerful these are and, therefore, it is worth investing more money in a model or another piece of technology that is better equipped to suit our learning objectives from the start and may be used for longer.

As far as the use of audiobooks is concerned, they are a very powerful tool for learning languages and a means to reconnect students with literature in various ways. As Burkey (2013) has pointed out, "the aural appreciation of story is the oldest form of literature, and voice captured on audiobook communicates an author's words in a way that recreates the oral tradition" (section "Into the future", para. 2). Thus, the project described above not only managed to successfully balance and integrate receptive and productive skills but was also an attempt to foster a blended type of 'pedagogy of reconnection' (Comber & Kamler, 2004), which is becoming more and more necessary as we progressively move away from what once was the core of our teaching.

---

[1]. I wish to thank Joe Dale, independent Modern Foreign Languages and technology consultant, for his advice and suggestions on the accessibility and promotion of this project.

References

Burkey, M. (2013, August 12). Sound literature: A guide to audiobooks for youth. *American Libraries*. Retrieved from http://www.americanlibrariesmagazine.org/article/sound-literature

Chace, W. M. (2009, September 1). The decline of the English department: How it happened and what could be done to reverse it. *The American Scholar.* Retrieved from http://theamericanscholar.org/the-decline-of-the-english-department/#.VCfa1RaOotE

Comber, B., & Kamler, B. (2004). Getting out of deficit: Pedagogies of reconnection. *Teaching Education, 15*(3), 293-310. doi:10.1080/1047621042000257225

De la Flor, C. (Ed.). (2008). *Relatos españoles contemporáneos, Colección Audiolibros* (book & CD-ROM). Madrid: Habla con Eñe.

De la Flor, C. (Ed.). (2010). *Relatos mexicanos, Colección Audiolibros* (book & CD-ROM). Madrid: Habla con Eñe.

De la Flor, C., & Paúl, M. (Eds). (2009). *Relatos del Río de la Plata, Colección Audiolibros* (book & CD-ROM). Madrid: Habla con Eñe.

18. Learning foreign languages with ClipFlair: Using captioning and revoicing activities to increase students' motivation and engagement

Rocío Baños[1] and Stavroula Sokoli[2]

Abstract

The purpose of this paper is to present the rationale and outcomes of ClipFlair, a European-funded project aimed at countering the factors that discourage Foreign Language Learning (FLL) by providing a motivating, easily accessible online platform to learn a foreign language through revoicing (e.g. dubbing) and captioning (e.g. subtitling). This paper will reflect on what has been achieved throughout the project and the challenges encountered along the way, in order to share our experience and inspire other FLL tutors in secondary and tertiary education. The focus is on the main outputs of the project: a) ClipFlair Studio, an online platform where users (both tutors and learners) can create, upload and access revoicing and captioning activities to learn a foreign language; b) ClipFlair Gallery, a library of resources containing over 350 activities to learn the 15 languages targeted in the project; and c) ClipFlair Social, an online community where learners, teachers and activity authors can share information.

Keywords: ClipFlair, audiovisual material, interactive, motivation, FLL, audiovisual translation, subtitling, dubbing.

---

1. University College London, United Kingdom; r.banos@ucl.ac.uk.

2. Universitat Pompeu Fabra, Spain; ssokoli@gmail.com.

How to cite this chapter: Baños, R., & Sokoli, S. (2015). Learning foreign languages with ClipFlair: Using captioning and revoicing activities to increase students' motivation and engagement. In K. Borthwick, E. Corradini, & A. Dickens (Eds), *10 years of the LLAS elearning symposium: Case studies in good practice* (pp. 203-213). Dublin: Research-publishing.net. doi:10.14705/rpnet.2015.000280

1. Context/rationale

The advantages of using audio-visual material in the foreign language (FL) classroom are widely acknowledged and have been explored by several scholars carrying out research in this field. Drawing on the existing literature, Talaván Zanón (2013) summarises the most relevant benefits of integrating audio-visual material in Foreign Language Learning (FLL): it introduces variety and creates an interactive and entertaining learning environment, thus increasing students' motivation; it provides exposure to non-verbal cultural elements and presents authentic linguistic and cultural aspects of communication in context; it is extremely flexible and can be adapted according to the needs of students and tutors; it promotes transferrable skills; and students can be easily encouraged to use this type of material when learning a language independently (pp. 52-53).

Regardless of how good or rich an audio-visual clip might be, we still need to find a way to integrate it naturally in our teaching, and to design tasks that engage learners and discourage passive viewing. Following this approach, some FL tutors have explored the advantages of integrating audio-visual translation modes in FLL. The benefits of this approach have been clearly discussed in the collective volumes published on this topic lately, especially in the case of subtitling (e.g. Incalcaterra McLoughlin, Biscio, & Ni Mhainnin, 2011). As was the case with the use of audio-visual material, no one seems to dispute the appropriateness and even the effectiveness of using audio-visual translation tasks (i.e. ask students to subtitle or revoice a short clip) to learn foreign languages. However, FL tutors who are not familiar with audio-visual translation might find these new approaches daunting, not only because they need to familiarise themselves with new terms used by experts (captioning, revoicing[1], audio description, dubbing, etc.), but also because they need to source the material and learn how to use the technology to make these activities possible, and they need to do so in the little time they can currently spare. As will be shown below, the ClipFlair project aims to solve some of these issues,

---

1. A definition of the terms revoicing and captioning is provided when discussing ClipFlair's conceptual framework.

having been designed bearing in mind the complex context in which FLL takes place and the needs of a wide-range of FL tutors and learners.

2. Aims and objectives

The ClipFlair project, funded by the European Commission, was launched in December 2011. It was designed with the main aim of enhancing interactivity when working with audio-visual material by providing a single platform where a wide community of FL tutors, learners and activity designers could interact. More specifically, the key aims of ClipFlair were to develop:

- a methodological framework for FLL through captioning and revoicing;

- an online platform (ClipFlair Studio) where users (both tutors and students) create, upload and access revoicing and captioning activities to learn a foreign language;

- a library of resources (ClipFlair Gallery) containing a wide range of audio-visual material, and over 300 activities to learn the 15 languages targeted in the project[1];

- an online community where learners, teachers and activity authors share information (ClipFlair Social).

3. What we did

In order to achieve the above-mentioned aims, the project mobilised ten institutions from eight European countries bringing together a diverse number of teachers and learners. Throughout the project, several institutions showed great interest in ClipFlair and joined the consortium as associated partners. ClipFlair

---

1. These were Arabic, Basque, Catalan, Chinese, English, Estonian, Greek, Irish, Japanese, Polish, Portuguese, Romanian, Russian, Spanish and Ukrainian.

could thus be considered a joint effort to share ideas and free interactive and innovative resources amongst the wider FLL community, especially in languages where limited material is available online.

3.1. ClipFlair's conceptual and methodological framework

Before being able to design the online platform and activities for FLL via captioning and revoicing, it was essential to establish the conceptual framework and the pedagogical methodology for this project. This involved researching the existing literature on FLL and audio-visual translation, and investigating relevant educational projects in this field. It soon became clear that one of the main tasks would be defining key terms to avoid misunderstandings and ensure consistency throughout the project. For instance, in ClipFlair, the terms 'captioning' and 'revoicing' are used as hyperonyms to refer to the insertion of text (captioning) or a voice recording (revoicing) in a clip with the purpose of learning a foreign language. Captioning involves adding subtitles, inserts and speech bubbles to a clip, for example, whereas revoicing involves adding a free commentary or narration to a clip, or dubbing it, i.e. making sure the dialogue fits with the lip movements of characters on screen.

During the development of the conceptual framework, project members contributed to establishing the following key aspects: types of learners targeted (teacher-driven, guided and independent learners), types of skills to be learned, guidelines to source audio-visual material, general guidelines for activity authors, pedagogical approaches and suppositions when using revoicing and captioning in FLL, etc. Discussions around these topics were essential to have a clear idea of what we wanted to achieve and, ultimately, to produce the specifications for the creation of the online platform (ClipFlair Studio). The purpose was to produce a very flexible and easy-to-use platform that could be integrated in a wide range of contexts, as well as to compile resources that could be reused or used as inspiration by FL tutors to work on a variety of skills and increase students' motivation. We also wanted to create a community feeling, which was achieved through the development of ClipFlair Social.

3.2. ClipFlair Studio and ClipFlair Social

The online platform, designed to be free, open source and with both online and offline access, needed to be developed from scratch, as a completely new and innovative product. The creation of the functional specifications of the platform, based on the above-mentioned educational specifications, was followed by the development of the alpha and beta versions of the platform. Both versions were tested by project members, who provided detailed feedback to developers. During testing, users were able to report all kinds of issues, from technical defects to suggestions for improvements in functionality, posting relevant messages[1] on the ClipFlair Social. Effective communication between project members was essential at this stage: less tech savvy members had to make sure developers understood how to implement the feedback given, and developers needed to make sure project members understood their limitations, considering the time and budget available. Through the development stages a great emphasis was placed on user experience with one of the main priorities being the user-friendliness of the platform. The aim was to ensure that the beta version, which would be tested by learners and tutors during the pilot phase, was as functional and user-friendly as possible. During the pilot phases, feedback was gathered both on the specific activity piloted and on the performance of ClipFlair Studio and/or ClipFlair Social. For example, as a result of the feedback provided, developers worked on enabling text directionality for Arabic, and implemented a feature that allowed loading clips locally in addition to using clips available online.

3.3. ClipFlair Gallery

In order to build a large library of resources to be used by the wider FLL community, guidelines to standardise the process were needed first. For the compilation of the video gallery[2], the issue of copyright was investigated and project members were informed about the type of licences videos should comply

---

1. http://social.clipflair.net/ > Contribute > Feedback on Social.

2. http://gallery.clipflair.net/video/

with (e.g. Attribution Non-Commercial Share-Alike, educational purpose licence under the Berne convention). A list of online websites where videos meeting these criteria could be downloaded was compiled, and project members were encouraged to upload as many relevant clips as possible, using the appropriate forum[1] in the ClipFlair Social to suggest material. A clip metadata form was filled in for each of the uploaded videos (to include the language of the clip, duration, description, genre, etc.), to ensure users will be able to search for videos at a later stage in a user-friendly way.

A similar process was followed for the creation of activities and the activity gallery[2]. Project members were involved in the design of over 350 activities for the 15 languages targeted in the project. Activities include media files, instructions for the completion of requested tasks, captioning and/or revoicing panels, and any additional text, image or media component deemed necessary by the authors. As with video clips, authors were requested to fill in a form providing necessary metadata such as the title of the activity, name of the author(s), keywords, aims, estimated time for completion of tasks, languages, level according to the Common European Framework (CEFR), skills acquired, mode of feedback to learners, etc. Activities were created through different stages of the project, and they were reviewed constantly by the own designers. In addition, all activities underwent a peer-review process. This was essential not only for quality assurance purposes, but also to have the opportunity to integrate the new features developed in ClipFlair Studio and the social network in existing activities.

4. Discussion

The ClipFlair project has resulted in a series of outcomes which can now be enjoyed by the wider FLL community. The most relevant outcomes and their impact will be discussed here.

---

1. http://social.clipflair.net/ > Contribute > Suggest Material

2. http://gallery.clipflair.net/activity/

ClipFlair's conceptual and methodological framework, which is available online[1], is crucial to understanding the principles that have guided the whole project. It is hoped that this document will be used as an additional resource by tutors and researchers wanting to investigate the use of audio-visual translation in FLL. One of the main challenges faced when developing the framework was reflecting the needs of all tutors and language learners, as well as the complex nature of audio-visual texts. The latter led us to suggest a further set of audio-visual skills, including watching, audio-visual speaking and audio-visual writing, since the four language learning skills as traditionally used seem to be too restrictive, leaving no room for audio-visual communication and multimodality. We categorised activities according to three types of learner response[2]: repeat, rephrase or react to the audio-visual material.

- Repeat: rendering the verbal part of the clip as literally as possible.

- Rephrase: free rendering or noticeable rewording of the text.

- React: producing a new communicative contribution in response to a previous one.

ClipFlair Studio, the online application to create and use FLL activities that involve captioning and revoicing, is one of the main outcomes of the project. Unlike other tools available for captioning and revoicing clips, ClipFlair Studio is free, very flexible and easy to use, and it provides all the necessary components in a single area. With a detailed online user guide[3] available in 12 languages and video tutorials explaining ClipFlair Studio basics, learning to create new activities and to use existing ones is very simple. FL tutors may use a ready-made activity as it is, adapt it to their needs or create their own, either using their own video or choosing one from the ClipFlair video gallery. Authors who wish to share their activities can upload them on the activity gallery to enrich it.

---

1. http://www.slideshare.net/ClipFlair/clipflair-conceptual-framework-and-pedagogical-methodology

2. This was important when designing an activity, as learners need to know what they are expected to do, or may wish to search a certain type of exercise.

3. http://social.clipflair.net/Help/Manual.aspx

Chapter 18

At the time of writing this paper, the gallery contains a wide range of video clips, images, and over 350 revoicing and captioning activities, covering all CEFR levels, to learn 19 languages. Thanks to the gathering of metadata for videos and activities mentioned above, tutors and learners can search the gallery to find activities or videos that suit their needs. It is expected that the number of activities, videos and languages will increase as more members join the ClipFlair community.

Figure 1. Example of an activity in ClipFlair (ClipFlair tutorial)

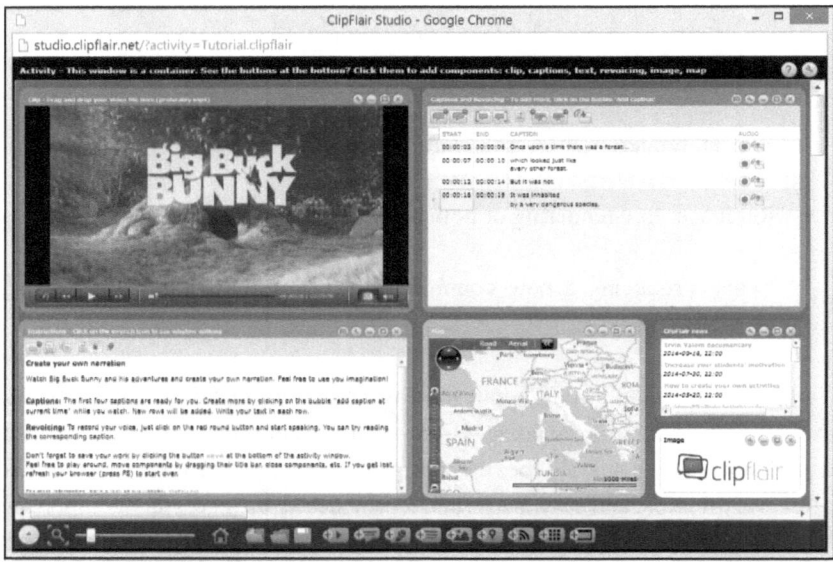

Each activity in the gallery has its own link which tutors can easily share with learners. Figure 1 shows a ClipFlair tutorial, whose URL is http://studio.clipflair.net/?activity=Tutorial.clipflair.

As can be seen when visiting ClipFlair Gallery, ClipFlair caters for different levels of participation, depending on the learner needs and level, from the minimum level of activity (e.g. watching a video, fill in the gaps in the subtitles) to the maximum (e.g. subtitling in L2 without a script). Some ClipFlair activities require learners to simulate the work of audio-visual translators (e.g. to subtitle[1] or dub a clip from one language to another, to subtitle within the same language for deaf and hard-of-hearing viewers[2], or to provide an audio description for blind and visually impaired viewers[3]), whereas others might not involve translation as such, but require learners to produce a text to be narrated at a later stage.

A single activity can promote the acquisition and reinforcement of several skills: for example, if students are asked to dub a clip with audio in the L2, they will be working on oral production and on listening comprehension, and increasing their cultural awareness and vocabulary at the same time. In addition, if some parts of the clip are muted, they will not only reproduce what they hear (e.g. repeat), but also create new content in the L2 (e.g. react). Tasks can be more or less time-consuming and may require more or less technical knowledge on the part of the learner.

Given that learning is a unique and individual process, the fact that learners learn at different paces is also taken into account: ClipFlair allows learners to follow instructions and repeat videos as many times as they need in order to complete an activity. However, since learning is also a social process, the platform also provides collaboration tools through ClipFlair Social including forums, groups and blogs to allow for different levels of learner involvement. At the time of writing this paper, ClipFlair Social has 1,400 registered members, and it is expected that this number will increase in the near future as more tutors and learners join the ClipFlair community.

As regards the feedback received from FL tutors and learners, it is worth mentioning the results of ClipFlair's pilot phase briefly. This phase lasted approximately one year and involved 37 tutors and 1,213 learners, who tested 84 language learning activities for 12 languages (English, Portuguese,

---

1. Subtitling activity example: http://studio.clipflair.net/?activity=1Waterloo-Cap-C1-ANY.clipflair.

2. Subtitling for the hard-of-hearing example: http://studio.clipflair.net/?activity=Yalom-Cap-B2-EN.clipflair.

3. Audio description example: http://studio.clipflair.net/?activity=VisitBritain-CapRev-C1-EN.clipflair.

Spanish, Arabic, Chinese, Catalan, Romanian, Polish, Basque, Irish, Estonian and Italian), mainly in higher and secondary education institutions. The fact that only 23% of the tutors reported experiencing technical issues is encouraging, especially considering that this was done on the beta version of the platform. Regarding learners' feedback, more than 80% found the activities used interesting and useful for language learning, and reported that they would like to work on similar activities to learn foreign languages. In addition, the majority considered the activity fun. Over 80% of the learners had no technical difficulties while using ClipFlair Studio, and a similar percentage considered it to be user-friendly. Although the survey reveals that the attractiveness of the interface could be improved (the answers were divided between 'attractive' and 'more or less attractive'), the overall response from students was very positive, with over 80% acknowledging having enjoyed working with ClipFlair.

During the pilot phase most activities were tested in class together with the teacher (70%), but the project has shown that the learning context where ClipFlair can be used is flexible. In the case of teacher-driven learners who follow a course with predefined units and lessons, the tutor can decide how learners can best use ClipFlair for activities integrated in the syllabus, as supplementary material, or otherwise (remedial work, voluntary work, further reference, etc.).

At the other end of the continuum, independent learners selecting and organising their own learning path, goals and strategies, are able to use ClipFlair activities freely, to modify and adapt them for their needs or even create their own.

5. Conclusion

Although the funding period for the ClipFlair project has drawn to an end, the platform will be maintained for at least five years and can be accessed for free. The aim of the ClipFlair consortium has been to consolidate and pave the way for future research, projects and applications to come, contributing with tangible results. We hope to have increased awareness and to have provided useful resources and a flexible and user-friendly platform to exploit the great potential of captioning and revoicing for FLL.

References

Incalcaterra McLoughlin, L., Biscio, M., & Ni Mhainnin, M. A. (Eds). (2011). *Audiovisual translation. Subtitles and subtitling: Theory and practice*. Bern: Peter Lang.
Talaván Zanón, N. (2013). *La subtitulación en el aprendizaje de lenguas extranjeras*. Barcelona: Octaedro.

Websites

ClipFlair Gallery: http://gallery.clipflair.net/
ClipFlair Social: http://social.clipflair.net/
ClipFlair Studio: http://studio.clipflair.net/
ClipFlair Website: http://clipflair.net/

19 FLAX: Flexible and open corpus-based language collections development

Alannah Fitzgerald[1], Shaoqun Wu[2], and María José Marín[3]

Abstract

In this case study we present innovative work in building open corpus-based language collections by focusing on a description of the open-source multilingual Flexible Language Acquisition (FLAX) language project, which is an ongoing example of open materials development practices for language teaching and learning. We present language-learning contexts from across formal and informal language learning in English for Academic Purposes (EAP). Our experience relates to Open Educational Resource (OER) options and Practices (OEP) which are available for developing and distributing online subject-specific language materials for uses in academic and professional settings. We are particularly concerned with closing the gap in language teacher training where competencies in materials development are still dominated by print-based proprietary course book publications. We are also concerned with the growing gap in language teaching practitioner competencies for understanding important issues of copyright and licencing that are changing rapidly in the context of digital and web literacy developments. These key issues are being largely ignored in the informal language teaching practitioner discussions and in the formal research into teaching and materials development practices.

Keywords: FLAX, corpora, MOOC, OER, OEP, open access, open-source software, open data, domain-specific language, legal English.

---

1. Concordia University Department of Education Montreal, Canada; alannahfitzgerald@gmail.com.

2. University of Waikato Department of Computer Science Hamilton, New Zealand; shaoqunyw@gmail.com.

3. Universidad de Murcia Departamento de Filologia Inglesa Murcia, Spain; mariajose.marin1@um.es.

How to cite this chapter: Fitzgerald, A., Wu, S., & Marin, M. J. (2015). FLAX: Flexible and open corpus-based language collections development. In K. Borthwick, E. Corradini, & A. Dickens (Eds), *10 years of the LLAS elearning symposium: Case studies in good practice* (pp. 215-227). Dublin: Research-publishing.net. doi:10.14705/rpnet.2015.000281

Chapter 19

1. Context/rationale

Corpus-based approaches for language learning, teaching and materials development have featured frequently in the research into Computer Assisted Language Learning (CALL) but they have yet to become mainstream practice in classroom-based language education. Accessibility remains a central issue whereby many existing corpus-based tools and resources are beyond the reach of most language learners and teachers. Restrictions stem from a combination of complex and often outdated user interface designs and still, in many cases, from subscription costs. Usability studies with corpus-based systems have also failed to materialise in the research and development trends from the growing body of literature dedicated to CALL.

Enter Massive Open Online Courses (MOOCs) and OERs where opportunities arise for the re-visioning and re-purposing of corpus-based approaches for the development of language support in online learning. In many ways this case study reflects our growing interest in online learning –an untapped educational environment that would appear to be a natural home for the uptake of web-based corpus tools and resources– where language support needs to be scaled for large numbers of users at minimal cost. It is our objective to bridge new contexts of online research, development and practice in open education with corpus-based approaches within traditional classroom-based language education. We are doing this by reusing open content and data to build domain-specific language collections with the FLAX system.

FLAX is defined as

> "an open-source software system designed to automate the production and delivery of interactive digital language collections [and language exercises. Source] material comes from digital libraries (language corpora, web data, open access (OA) publications, open educational resources) for a virtually endless supply of authentic [linguistic examples] in context. With simple interface designs, FLAX has been designed so that non-expert users –language teachers, language learners, subject specialists,

instructional design and e-learning support teams– can build their own collections [of language, as well as their own exercises based on a wide pool of linguistic material].

The FLAX software can be freely downloaded to build [language] collections with any text-based content and supporting audio-visual material, for both online and classroom use" (Fitzgerald, 2014, para. 3).

This case study will provide an ongoing example of the collaborative development of the Law Collections on the FLAX website for supporting formal and informal English language learning with corpus-based approaches.

2. Aims and objectives

- To demonstrate how subject-specific language collections can be built with the FLAX open-source software for uses across formal and informal education, as exemplified by the Law Collections development on the FLAX website.

- To engage language teaching and research practitioners in the design process of subject-specific collections development in FLAX, and to research the efficacy of these collections for uptake by learners and teachers in MOOCs as well as in traditional classroom-based language learning.

- To share a methodology for distributing openly available tools and resources for subject-specific language education.

In a research and development project with FLAX for building subject-specific language learning collections, we sourced relevant open content in the area of socio-legal English, including the 8.85 million-word British Law Reports Corpus (BLaRC) (Figure 1), MOOC lectures, OA law journal and PhD theses publications (Fitzgerald, Wu, & Barge, 2014).

Chapter 19

Figure 1. BLaRC in the FLAX Law Collections

Table 1. Open resources featured in and linked to the FLAX Law Collections (Fitzgerald, 2014, section "Law Collections in FLAX")

Type of Resource	Number and Source of Collection Resources
Open Access Law research articles	40 Articles (DOAJ – Directory of Open Access Journals[1], with Creative Commons licenses for the development of derivatives).
MOOC lecture transcripts and videos (streamed via YouTube and Vimeo)	4 MOOC Collections: English Common Law (University of London with Coursera)[2], Age of Globalization (Texas at Austin with edX)[3], Copyright Law (Harvard with edX)[4], Environmental Politics and Law (OpenYale).
Podcast audio files and transcripts (OpenSpires)	15 Lectures (Oxford Law Faculty and the Centre for Socio-Legal Studies).
PhD Law thesis writing	50-70 EThOS Theses[5] (sections: abstracts, introductions, conclusions) at the British Library (Open Access but not licensed as Creative Commons – permission for reuse granted by participating Higher Education Institutions).

1. http://doaj.org/

2. https://www.coursera.org/course/engcomlaw

3. https://www.edx.org/course/utaustinx/utaustinx-ut-3-02x-age-globalization-2626

4. http://copyx.org/

5. http://ethos.bl.uk/Home.do;jsessionid=4F2E6E1673362D6ED04702DFA665C081

BLaRC	8.85 million-word corpus derived from free legal sources at the British and Irish Legal Information Institute (BAILII)[1] aggregation website.
Legal Terms List	A legal English vocabulary derived from the BLaRC using two Automatic Term Recognition Methods.
FLAX Wikipedia English	Linking in a reformatted version of Wikipedia (English version), providing key terms and concepts as a powerful gloss resource for the Law Collections.
FLAX Learning Collocations	Linking in lexico-grammatical phrases from the British National Corpus (BNC)[2] of 100 million words, the British Academic Written English corpus (BAWE)[3] of 2500 pieces of assessed university student writing from across the disciplines, and a re-formatted Wikipedia corpus in English of approximately 2.5 million articles.
FLAX Web Phrases	Linking in a reformatted Google n-gram corpus (English version) containing 380 million five-word sequences drawn from a vocabulary of 145,000 words.

3. What we did: developing demonstration open Law Collections in FLAX

The following sections outline how we built the Law Collections in FLAX and key aspects of their functionality for language teaching. The features described offer a model of how FLAX can be used. The approach is fully automated and can be applied to any FLAX language collection.

Functionality. Ease of navigation and attractive, simple user interfaces are central to FLAX. Iterations of the FLAX software to create your own stand-alone FLAX server and to implement the FLAX MOODLE module (within the MOODLE virtual learning environment) are available for download on the FLAX website. With the development of the FLAX MOODLE module, new and simpler teacher interfaces were developed to move away from the more complex librarian interfaces used in the standard Greenstone digital library software, which the FLAX open-source software is an extension of (Witten, Wu, & Yu, 2011).

1. http://www.bailii.org/

2. http://www.natcorp.ox.ac.uk/

3. http://www.coventry.ac.uk/research/research-directory/art-design/british-academic-written-english-corpus-bawe/

Chapter 19

The free *Book of FLAX* e-book, available on the FLAX website, tells you everything you need to know about building your own interactive FLAX collections featuring game-based activities like the one shown in Figure 2 below. A series of FLAX training videos in Chinese and English are also available on the FLAX website, with the latter featured on the Teacher Training Videos[1] website.

Figure 2. FLAX Collocations Guessing Game learner interface populated by the BNC corpus

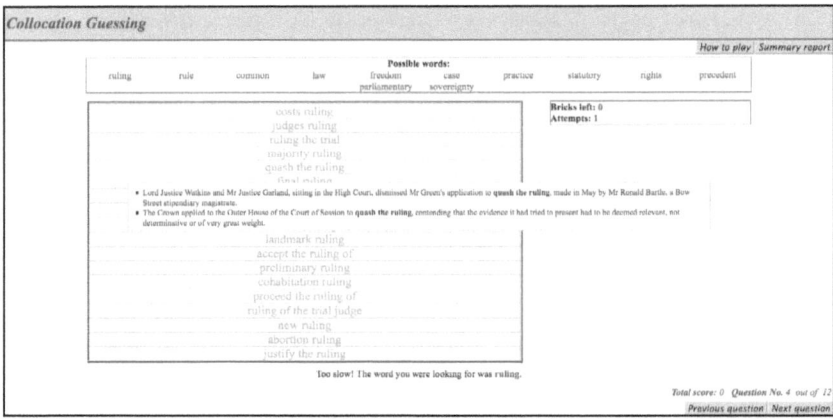

Building open language collections in FLAX. Available on the FLAX website are completed collections and on-going collections being developed by registered users. All resources are pre-processed before being built into FLAX collections. For example, lecture transcripts and OA publications undergo simple editing, including division into subsections, and are reformatted into manageable chunks as HTML files to decrease the cognitive load for learners when listening and viewing.

How the open datasets are combined and used in the FLAX user interface. FLAX links relevant tools and reusable resources into streamlined online

---
1. http://teachertrainingvideos.com/

interfaces for language teachers and learners. By reusable resources, this can mean one of two things: those that are openly licenced, and those for which we have gained permission to use for non-commercial purposes. For example, some datasets used in FLAX (the BNC, the BAWE corpus, and the Google web dump n-grams corpus) have restrictive licences, but the open datasets (Wikipedia, the BLaRC, OER, and OA publications) have non-restrictive licences for language resource development purposes for uses in education and research.

In the formatting stage of pre-processing documents for inclusion in the Law Collections in FLAX, licences originating from the different OER and OA data sources have been reflected accurately in the FLAX system to show the different permissions for reuse by end users. Built into the FLAX software when building collections is an acknowledgement message highlighted in blue for the collections builders to show that they are aware of the licencing permissions of the different resources they are using to make collections [*"Before you include any document in your collection, please ensure that you have copyright permission to do so"*]. However, actual practice with understanding and reusing the variety of copyrighted resources available online is not necessarily something with which language teachers are familiar or confident in handling. This is why we are building public collections with language teachers and learners on the FLAX website to demonstrate, and document through our research, best open educational and design practices for the development of language collections with the FLAX open-source software.

Video streaming and part-of-speech tagging. Audio-visual resources in the form of lectures and podcasts can be either embedded directly into the FLAX software or are streamed through well-known third party providers such as YouTube and Vimeo.

Wikipedia Miner toolkit. FLAX connects to the open-source Wikipedia Miner toolkit, also developed at the University of Waikato, to extract key concepts and their definitions from Wikipedia articles to assist with reading and vocabulary in subject-specific areas as seen in Figure 3. Key concepts and their definitions are extracted from Wikipedia articles and are linked to documents in FLAX collections. For example, *Factortame litigation, European Communities Act 1972 (UK), Thorburn v Sunderland City Council, Human Rights Act 1998, Supremacy (European Union Law)*, are identified as related topics in Wikipedia to provide a broader context for understanding the English Common Law MOOC sub-collection in FLAX, and a definition for *parliamentary sovereignty* is also extracted.

Figure 3. FLAX augmented text interface with wikify function in Law MOOC Collections

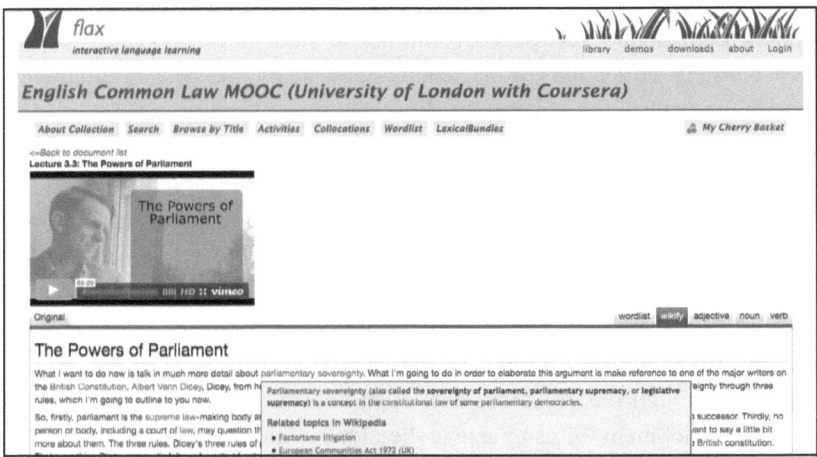

Search capabilities. Search queries in FLAX are highlighted in yellow for ease of recognition and can contain more than one word. For phrase searching, a query can be enclosed by quotation marks; for example, *"doctrine of precedent"* returns sentences containing this exact phrase, while *doctrine of precedent* returns sentences that contain these three words and associated words in any order, e.g. *this idea of the binding doctrine of precedent.*

Keywords and word lists. "The development of *wordlist* and *keyword* interfaces [in FLAX] also allows learners to analyse the range of vocabulary used in a specified document, including the General Service List (West, 1953), the Academic Word List (AWL) by Coxhead (2000) and Off-list [topic-specific] words" (Fitzgerald, 2013, section "Open Linguistic Support in the Context of Formal and Informal EAP", para. 4). Words can be sorted alphabetically or by frequency; in either case, frequency in the corpus is shown alongside the word.

Collocations. It is possible to focus on lexical collocations with noun based structures noun + noun, adjective + noun, noun + of + noun, verb + noun, verb + preposition + noun, adjective + to + verb and adjective + preposition + noun as seen in Figure 4 because they are the most important and useful patterns for second language learners of subject-specific language.

Figure 4. Collocations in Law Collections
         linked to FLAX Learning Collocations (Wikipedia) collection

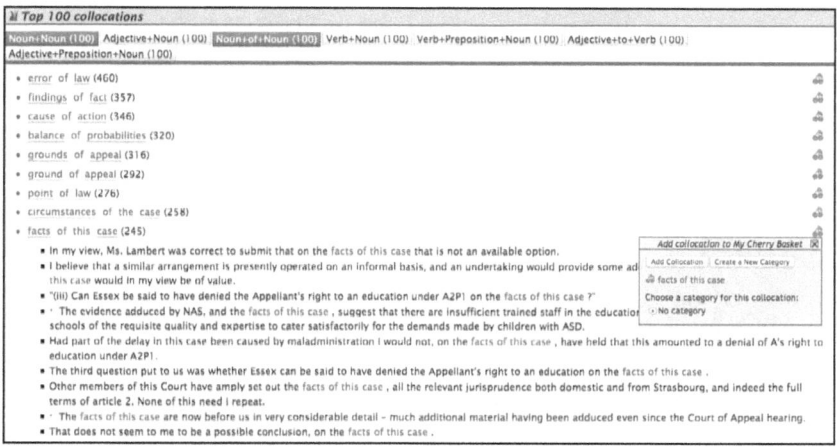

The Cherry Basket. By clicking on the cherry icon, also shown in Figure 4, users can go through the collections, selecting examples of language they wish to store and retrieve. By clicking on the blue hyperlinked words in the subject-specific collections, FLAX will link to a larger collocations database with the BNC, BAWE and Wikipedia corpora.

3.1. Who is using the open Law Collections in FLAX?

Following on from earlier work with the FLAX project into second language learning in the context of MOOCs (Fitzgerald, Wu, & Witten, 2014), we are currently investigating how the Law Collections in FLAX are being reused in the MOOCs listed earlier in this case study in Table 1 and in formal classroom-based language learning and translation contexts. The initial collections design work with language teachers at Queen Mary University of London focused on sourcing open resources that would be of relevance to their pre-sessional EAP law cohorts and more specifically with their postgraduate law students who require language support on their critical thinking and writing in-sessional programme. At the Universidad de Murcia in Spain, legal English translation students are reusing the English Common Law MOOC collection in FLAX to mine key lexico-grammatical patterns and prepare a class presentation and follow-on essay on the differences between the civil and common law systems.

3.2. Research with the open Law Collections in FLAX

To date, we have made the *English Common Law* and the *Age of Globalization* MOOC collections in FLAX available to 35,000+ registered learners in over a hundred different countries. We are reusing OER research instruments (surveys, interview and think aloud protocols) from the OER Research Hub[1] research bank based at the UK Open University to collect data on the following revised OER hypotheses[2] for language education using the FLAX collections in informal online learning and traditional classroom-based learning:

- *Hypothesis A*: use of OER language collections leads to improvement in student performance and satisfaction.

- *Hypothesis E*: use of OER for developing language collections leads to critical reflection by language educators, with improvement in their practice.

---

1. http://oerresearchhub.org/

2. Revised from Fitzgerald (2013, section "Multi-site Research into Developing Open Linguistic Support", para. 2).

- *Hypothesis K*: informal means of assessment are motivators to learning with OER language collections.

- *Hypothesis H*: informal learners adopt a variety of techniques to compensate for the lack of formal language support.

- *Hypothesis I*: open education acts as a bridge to formal language education, and is complementary, not competitive, with it.

4. Discussion

In terms of detailed feedback on the FLAX system with regards to using the Law Collections, the face-to-face research contexts are likely to yield more reliable findings into the actual efficacy of the system for impacting language learning. This will involve controlled and experimental groups to discern the impact of the FLAX system on learner writing and vocabulary acquisition for legal English through qualitative discourse analysis approaches. However, the type of data we can collect from MOOC learners will be quantitative. MOOC survey questions are matched to the OER research hypotheses to identify learners' perceptions of and use of the FLAX MOOC collections to support vocabulary, reading and listening comprehension of course content and for instances of language transfer into course discussions and peer-reviewed writing.

5. Conclusion

FLAX is committed to opening access in English language education through digital innovation. The FLAX system's capabilities for building language collections with comprehensive facilities for search and retrieval, and customised interactive learning of key subject terms and concepts, addresses the needs of both native and non-native speakers of English who are interested in engaging deeply with open subject-specific resources in English from the OER and OA movements. Furthermore, learners benefit from the enhancement of these open resources with FLAX's affordances for linking in datasets derived from massive online sources, namely Wikipedia and Google, and from large pre-formatted research corpora such as the BNC, the BLaRC and the BAWE.

Acknowledgements. We would like to thank the OER Research Hub, the Global OER Graduate Network, and The International Research Foundation (TIRF) for English Language Education Doctoral Dissertation Grant, for funding this research collaboration between the FLAX project at the University of Waikato in New Zealand, the Department of Education at Concordia University in Canada, and the Departamento de Filologia Inglesa, Universidad de Murcia in Spain.

References

Coxhead, A. (2000). A new academic word list. *TESOL Quarterly, 34*(2), 213-238. Reprinted in 2007 in Corpus linguistics by W. Teubert & R. Krishnamurthy (Eds), *Critical concepts in linguistics* (pp. 123-149). Oxford, England: Routledge. doi:10.2307/3587951

Fitzgerald, A. (2013, March 18). Educating in beta. *OER Research Hub*. Retrieved from http://oerresearchhub.org/2013/03/18/educating-in-beta/

Fitzgerald, A. (2014, October 6). Wow! The FLAX language system – So much open data. *TOETOE Technology for Open English - Toying with Open E-resources ('tɔɪtɔɪ)*. Retrieved from http://alannahfitzgerald.org/2014/10/06/vici-competition/

Fitzgerald, A., Wu, S., & Barge, M. (2014). Investigating an open methodology for designing domain-specific language collections. In S. Jager, L. Bradley, E. J. Meima, & S. Thouësny (Eds), *CALL Design: Principles and Practice; Proceedings of the 2014 EUROCALL Conference, Groningen, The Netherlands* (pp. 88-95). Dublin: Research-publishing.net. doi:10.14705/rpnet.2014.000200

Fitzgerald, A., Wu, S., & Witten, I. H. (2014). Second language learning in the context of MOOCs. *Proceedings of the 6th International Conference on Computer Supported Education* (pp. 354-359).

Witten, I. H., Wu, S., & Yu, X. (2011). Linking digital libraries to courses with particular application to language learning. *Proceedings of the 3rd International Conference on Computer Supported Education, Volume 1, Noordwijkerhout, Netherlands, 6-8 May, 2011* (pp. 5-14).

West, M. (1953). *A general service list of English words*. London: Longman, Green & Co.

FLAX website resource links

FLAX (Flexible Language Acquisition) project website: http://flax.nzdl.org

FLAX Age of Globalization MOOC collection (University of Texas at Austin): http://flax.nzdl.org/greenstone3/flax?a=fp&sa=collAbout&c=lawlecture&if=

FLAX British Law Reports Corpus (BLaRC) collection: http://flax.nzdl.org/greenstone3/flax?a=fp&sa=collAbout&c=BlaRC&if=

FLAX English Common Law MOOC collection (London University with Coursera): http://flax.nzdl.org/greenstone3/flax?a=fp&sa=collAbout&c=englishcommonlaw&if=

FLAX Learning Collocations Wikipedia English collection: http://tinyurl.com/nrc4or5

FLAX training videos: https://www.youtube.com/user/FlaxLanguageLearning/featured

Name index

Abbott, Chris 102
Alcarazo, Noelia 199
Alevizou, Panagiota 28, 29
Anderson, Terry 114
Arias-McLaughlin, Ximena 102

Baker, Will 112, 114
Baños, Rocío vii, 6, 203
Barge, Martin 217, 226
Bayne, Siân 114, 115
Beard, Jeffrey L. 34, 39
Beaven, Tita vii, 4, 5, 77, 79, 87
Bescond, G. 55
Biscio, Marie 204, 213
Borthwick, Kate v, xiii, 1
Brick, Billy vii, 4, 21
Britt, Virginia G. 34, 39
Brooks, Lindsay 187, 192
Burkey, Mary 201, 202

Camilleri, Anthony F. 79, 87
Camillini, Simona 124
Carr, Nicola 167, 172
Carter, Ronald 118, 126
Casserly, Catherine M. 78, 87
Cervi-Wilson, Tiziana viii, 4, 21
Chace, William M. 194, 202
Chan, Anthony 34, 39
Chavis, David M. 177, 184
Childs, Mark 61, 62, 66
Comas-Quinn, Anna xiii
Comber, Barbara 201, 202
Conole, Gráinne xv, 28, 29
Corradini, Erika v, xiii, 1
Couros, Alec 179, 180, 184
Coxhead, Averil 223, 226
Crombie, Margaret A. 95, 101, 102
Crookall, David 160, 161
Csikszentmihalyi, Mihaly 129, 132, 137

Dale, Joe 201
De la Flor, Clara 196, 202
Dickens, Alison v, xiii, 1, 111, 115
Downes, Stephen 66
Dron, Jon 114
Dyck, Jennifer L. 34, 39

Edirisingha, Palitha 112, 115
Efron, Sara Efrat 160, 161
Ehlers, Ulf Daniel 79, 87
Ellis, Robert 121, 126
Ellis, Rod 141, 149

Fayard, Nicole 14, 19
Fayram, Jo 102
Fell, Courtney Paige 24, 30
Fitzgerald, Alannah viii, 6, 215, 217, 218, 223, 224, 226
Fregona, C. 17, 19

Gallardo, Matilde 102
García, Oscar 199
Gauntlett, David 132, 133, 134, 137
Gazeley, Z. 55
Gilchrist, Graham 111, 115

Godard, Jean-Luc 123
Godwin-Jones, Robert 24, 30, 49, 55
Goodyear, Peter 121, 126
Guilbaud, Benoît vi, 5, 6, 175, 177, 184
Guth, Sarah 47, 48, 49, 54, 55

Habib, L. 102
Hall, Wendy 2
Hamby, L. 17, 19
Hamilton-Hart, Julien 119, 126
Heiser, Sarah 102
Helm, Francesca 47, 48, 49, 54, 55
Hendriks, Maaike 109, 115
Hill, Jenny 102
Howell, Holly 78, 87
Hoyle, Michelle A. 66
Hugo, Victor 122
Hummel, Hans 109, 115
Hurtado Albir, Amparo 164
Hutz, Matthias 148, 149

Iiyoshi, Toru 78, 87
Incalcaterra McLoughlin, Laura 204, 213

Jimes, Cynthia 78, 87
Jones, Jane 102

Kamler, Barbara 201, 202
King, Alison 16, 19
Kiss, Tamas 48, 49, 56
Koper, Rob 109, 115
Kreutner, Edith viii, 5, 139

Kukulska-Hulme, Agnes 22, 24, 30
Kumaravadivelu, B. 45, 49, 55
Kumar, M. S. Vijay 78, 87

Laurillard, Diana 112, 115
Lee, Mark J. W. 34, 39
LeLoup, Jean W. 186, 192
Liddicoat, Anthony J. 52, 55
Lister, Pen 17, 19
Littlejohn, Andrew 160, 161
Lloyd, M. 55
Lopez-Vera, B. 55
Lorenzo-Zamorano, Susana viii, 6, 193
Luber, Elise S. 34, 39
Lubke, Jennifer K. 34, 39

MacKinnon, Teresa ix, 4, 57, 61, 64, 66
Marín, María José ix, 6, 215
McKinney, Dani 34, 39
McMillan, David W. 177, 184
Middleton-Detzner, Clare 78, 87
Motzo, Anna ix, 5, 89

Nie, Ming 112, 115
Nijakowska, Joanna 102
Ni Mhainnin, Maire Aine 204, 213
Norris, John M. 141, 149

O'Bannon, Blanche W. 34, 39
O'Dowd, Robert 46, 56
Olvera Lobo, María Dolores 163, 172
Orsini-Jones, Marina vi, 4, 43, 44, 47, 50, 55
Ortega, Lourdes 141, 149

Name index

Oxford, Rebecca L. 160, 161

Pannekeet, Kees 109, 115
Paúl, Mar 196, 202
Pawlowski, Jan 79, 87
Penet, Jean-Christophe x, 4, 67
Penman, Christine x, 5, 117
Perkins, David 54, 56
Petrides, Lisa 78, 87
Pettiward, J. 17, 19
Pibworth, L. 55
Ponterio, Robert 186, 192

Quattrocchi, Debora x, 5, 89

Race, Phil 109, 115
Ravid, Ruth 160, 161
Roed, Jannie 102
Rolińska, Ania xi, 5, 127
Rosell-Aguilar, Fernando xi, 4, 31, 32, 33, 34, 37, 39
Rossi, Nerino 44
Ross, Jen 114, 115

Sadoux, Marion vi, 4, 11
Salmon, Gilly K. 112, 115
Scarino, Angela 52, 55
Schneider, E. 102
Schulz, Renate A. 148, 149
Seely Brown, John 58, 64, 65, 66
Sharma, Pete 186, 192
Shor, Ira 133, 135, 137
Siemens, George 180, 184
Silipo, S. 102

Simon, Edwige F. 24, 30
Smith, Marshall S. 78, 87
Sokoli, Stavroula xi, 6, 203
Stollhans, Sascha xi, 6, 185
Swain, Merrill 186, 187, 190, 192

Tait, Alan 79, 88
Talaván Zanón, Noa 204, 213
Tandy, Vic 44
Thomas, Douglas 58, 64, 65, 66
Thouësny, Sylvie xiii
Tocalli-Beller, Agustina 187, 192

Ulmer, Gregory L. 129, 137
Ushioda, Ema 68, 69, 75

VanDerPloeg, Laura S. 160, 161
Vilar Beltrán, Elina 102
Vine, Juliet xii, 5, 163
Vygotsky, Lev Semyonovich 180, 184

Warschauer, Mark 176, 184
Watson, Julie vii, 5, 105, 110, 111, 112, 114, 115
Weller, Martin 64, 66, 80, 88
Weninger, Csilla 48, 49, 56
West, M. 223, 227
Wiazemsky, Anne 123
Wiley, David A. 110, 115
Winchester, Susanne 102
Witten, Ian H. 219, 224, 226
Wright, Vicky xvi
Wu, Shaoqun xii, 6, 215, 217, 219, 224, 226

Yeh, Aidan 5
Yeh, Aiden xii, 151
Yus, Francisco 46, 56
Yu, Xiaofeng 219, 226

Zerón, Ana 122
Zola, Emile 120

www.ingramcontent.com/pod-product-compliance
Lightning Source LLC
Chambersburg PA
CBHW022005160426
43197CB00007B/280